OUTDOOR GAS GRIDDLE COOKBOOK

Best Recipes With Color Photos and Super Easy Directions.

RECIPELY.NET

COPYRIGHT

TABLE OF CONTENTS

Introduction

Hello readers, my name is TODD STONE, I am an American cook, and I am part of a group of American cooks, chefs, and amateurs, called (RECIPELY.NET) our group which aims to share their passion and help people with their experience. Our long experience concerns a way of cooking that is part of our culture and our enjoyment: gas griddle cooking.

With many years of experience behind me, I thought it would be useful to share it with all of you. Only in this way would it be possible for me to allow as many people as possible to make the most of the potential of outdoor gas griddle, without getting lost among manuals, various blogs and resources scattered on the net.

This text, therefore, in addition to be a recipe book, is intended to be an easy guide to always carry with you.

Thanks to this guide you will discover that it is possible to cook delicious recipes with gas griddle, as well as that it is possible to cook any type of recipe with this tool. Furthermore, you will rediscover the pleasure of a nice barbecue with friends.

Anyway, in this guide you will find all the useful information in order to be able to maintain and clean the gas outdoor griddle, how to use it and season it for the first time, reference tables of cooking times and anything else that will allow you to use it to the best.

In addition to all the information present, it is possible to find on the site (RECIPELY.NET) lots of other information on recipes, on grids such as manuals, tricks and a community of people who exchange advice.

Thanks to these tips of mine, you will be able to go from beginner to master grill in no time! I also started practically from scratch and went on to be an expert grill cook! On the other hand, as an old and famous saying goes: "Rome was built in a day"!

And I am pretty sure you will be successful with your outdoor grill session"

How to cook with an
outdoor gas griddle

Which better way to start this guide with a little very useful distinction and some good advice about? All that I have learned when I decided to buy an outdoor grill was to understand what kind of cooking, I could use depending on the dishes I wanted to prepare.

What I want you to know, in fact, first, is that you can have two different kinds of cooking with a gas griddle: direct and indirect.

Let's see how these cooking types of work.

DIRECT COOKING

I say to you that direct cooking is perfect for small cuts of food or for foods that don't require a cooking time of more than 20 minutes.

For direct cooking, light all the burners with the lid open. Once the burners are all lit, set them to the desired temperature and close the lid. Preheat the grill for about 5 to 10 minutes. Then place the food directly on the cooking grid, close the lid and proceed with cooking.

Cooking takes place by direct radiation of heat and by conduction of the material of which the grill is made. With direct cooking, very high temperatures are reached, even over 662° F, temperatures that allow you to quickly cook small cuts of meat or fish.

The peculiar characteristic of this type of cooking is the famous grill marks or the characteristic streaks that the grill leaves when the food is in direct contact with the heat.

The main difficulty of direct cooking is essentially the flames. These flare-ups are due to the grease in the food which, when melting, drips onto the burner flames. The solution to this problem is the correct use of the lid. In fact, it will be enough to close the lid to limit the access of oxygen in order to immediately extinguish the flames.

INDIRECT COOKING

All I have learned with my experience is that could be another non-traditional cooking method! With using this cooking method, the grill works as if it was a convection oven. Therefore, it is excellent for roasts, bread, desserts, leavened products, pizza, and all types of cooking that you usually do in the oven.

To proceed with this type of cooking I recommend to light all the burners with the lid open. Once the ignition is complete, set the burners to maximum temperature and then close the lid. Let the grill preheat for about 5 to 10 minutes. Turn off the center burners and place the food on top of the unlit burners. Lower the lit burners to medium heat to reduce the temperature and close the lid.

So, to cook indirectly you need to divide the two areas of your grill in half: on one side the burner on and on the other a completely free area with the burner off.

The food is cooked on the opposite side of the lit burner and cooking continues with the lid closed. By closing the lid, we will therefore have a closed cooking system, where the heat does not directly affect the food, but thanks to the displacement of air that circulates inside the cooking chamber, thus cooking delicately, indirectly and by heat convention.

Indirect cooking takes longer than direct cooking but allows you to cook large pieces of meat without running the risk of burning the outside and, at the same time, cooking the inside flawlessly.

To complete this type of cooking in the best possible way, it is essential to have a digital food probe thermometer in order to constantly check the temperature of the food you are cooking.

How to use your
outdoor gas griddle

A LITTLE GUIDE ON HOW TO CONDITION THE GRIDDLE FOR THE FIRST TIME

A very important thing for me is to learn how to condition your gas grill for the first time. from here I understood that all subsequent performances will then depend! And I'm right here with this guide to avoid making you make this mistake! Do you know how many of my friends have fallen for it?

For this, here is my mini guide for you to condition your grill for the first time!

The first thing to remember to use the gas griddle for the first time is if it uses soapstone for cooking food, it is essential to sprinkle the surface with cooking oil and remember to carefully clean the residues of grease and food; another important thing does not subject the stone to sudden changes in temperature, for example, by pouring cold water on the hot griddle.

So, to prevent foods from sticking to the griddle for the first time, dispersing all their juices, and inevitably ruining themselves during cooking, you can use these two tips:

1. If you have just purchased a griddle, wash it in salted water and dry it thoroughly.

2. Grease it on both sides with vegetable oil or lard and leave it to act for at least 24 hours so that it is absorbed. If possible, however, it is better to let two- or three-days pass. The oil has a dual function:

*   makes it more elastic and therefore resistance to thermal changes

*   fills the natural micro cavities of the stone, preventing them from being occupied during cooking by other elements (residues of cooking embers, etc.).

3. The residual fat must then be eliminated with a paper towel.

4. Spread the griddles with butter and oil before heating it

5. Heat the cooking grill to perfection. Furthermore, the temperature at which you have to heat the plates or grills must always be high. However, remember that the first time must be heated gradually, making sure that the fire is uniform over the entire surface to prevent it from expanding to form small cracks, which would compromise its subsequent use.

HOW TO CONDITION YOUR GRILL IN GENERAL

After my invaluable tips on how to condition for the first time, I could not avoid to dedicate a section how to you to condition your outdoor grill in general!

Conditioning is very important for the purpose of protecting them from attack by rust and making them non-stick during cooking.

I want you to know that in addition to the importance of this procedure also the way to do it.

If I close my eyes and think back to when I was a little boy, when I wasn't cooking yet, my parents come to mind in front of the open stove and there, on the fire, a cast iron plate. I see my mom picking on my dad first because she got the food attacked. It seemed like a tragedy!

If a few years ago you asked me for advice on buying a cast iron griddle, what do you think I would have replied? Then I grew up, I started cooking a little something myself and I learned a few things. Among these is just how to cook with cast iron and be happy at the same time.

Cast iron is one of the best materials for cooking, but for it to perform at its best you need to take some precautions and I'm here for this reason!

Conditioning is a process that affects cast iron utensils (not only plates and grills, but also pots and pans). Its purpose is to protect them from rust and to make them non-stick during cooking.

The cast iron must be cleaned, covered with a very thin layer of fat (animal or vegetable) and put in the oven.

Thanks to the heat, a chemical process called polymerization is accelerated which transforms the layer of fat making it hard and resistant. This creates a barrier to protect the cast iron.

Th best fats to use, in my opinion, are the so-called polyunsaturated fats. Without going into detail, these are fats that have multiple carbon double bonds ($C = C$) within their molecular structure. The greater the number of these bonds, the greater the cross-linking of the polymer (although it must be borne in mind that the higher the level of unsaturation, the more fragile the polymer is).

In principle, any fat with the characteristics described above is fine and, in fact, each person has their favorite or the one they are best with. Some use animal fats such as lard, lard or bacon fat, others use vegetable fats (the various seed oils, avocado oil, canola oil, etc.).

In summary, all the outdoor gas griddle cast irons must be cleaned, covered with a very thin layer of fat (animal or vegetable) and put in the oven.

In this way I am sure that the cast iron will be protected and your recipes will be perfect to say the least!

OUTDOOR GAS GRIDDLE ACCESSORIES

Ah, the accessories, how would I do without? In my opinion, having many accessories is equivalent to preparing delicious dishes!

So, don't be afraid to buy all the necessary for "accessorize" your outdoor grill!

Here you are all the accessories for your gas griddle. All these accessories will be listed below and what they are for.

- **VERTICAL BRAZIER.** It is a tank, generally made of steel or cast iron, and therefore capable of withstanding high temperatures, formed by a vertical plate and a front grill. It is mainly used for cooking on the spit. The advantage of the vertical brazier is given by the fact that the radiation coming from the side avoids burning the food with flames. Furthermore, the dripping fats do not end up on the embers, but are collected in a dripping pan, so that they can be recovered and used as a condiment. It allows greater control of the cooking of dishes but cannot be used for all types of food.

- **HORIZONTAL BRAZIER.** It is a surface formed by a grid, which can be in steel or cast iron, which has metal rods close together to allow support to the embers, the correct flow of air to the fuel and the fall of the ashes into a special container, placed under the same grid.

- **COOKING GRILL.** It tends to be a grill, made of metal and very rarely of cast iron, used to display food directly on the heat source. It is equipped with insulated handles, which are used to regulate, in safety, the distance of the food from the heat source. There are two types of grids: normal ones and those suitable for collecting juices. Some grills are book-like, so you can enclose the food between the two grids, making it easier to cook food from both sides.

- **PLATES OR STONES.** They are hobs that are used as alternatives to the grill. They are usually made of soapstone or lava, materials that have a high thermal inertia. Many plates are also made of cast iron. The plates are first heated over direct heat and then used to cook and keep food warm. They allow you to cook food without adding seasonings, but you must pay attention to foods that are too fatty, because the fat could drip and end up directly on the grill.

- **SPIT OR ROTISSERIE.** It is a metal rod that rotates around its own axis, whose movement can be activated both manually and through an electric motor. The food to be cooked is skewered inside the spit and then blocked by mobile forks. They are usually placed on special supports. The distance from the embers is adjustable and, usually, they are placed on the sides of the hob.

- **UNIVERSAL PAN.** It is a special tray, generally made of stainless steel, which is placed on the spit to collect the cooking juices of the various foods.

- **ASH COLLECTOR.** It is a metal collector, often in the form of a drawer or box, which is located under the brazier and serves to collect the combustion residues. It is usually found in charcoal, pellet, or wood-burning gas griddle.

- **SIDE SUPPORTS.** They are structures, which can be equipped with hollows, holes, wings or protrusions, useful for positioning the grids, plates or skewers. They are placed at a variable distance, and depending on the cooking, from the embers.

- **SCREENS.** They are vertical structures closed on three sides and open only in the central position. They have the purpose of protecting the surface containing the embers and the cooking surface from the wind, but they are also useful as a spark arrester and splash guard. In many gas griddle the screens also incorporate the side supports.

- **BASEMENT.** The base is a support structure that can be either fixed or mobile. The purpose of the base is to be able to position the hob at an ideal height for cooking. As for fixed gas griddle, the material they are made of is usually building material such as concrete, stones and bricks. As for mobile gas griddle, it is usually made of wood or metal, it is equipped with wheels and special stops to ensure its stability.

- **COOKER HOOD.** It is an optional structure, which has the same shape as the hoods used in the kitchen. It can be made of metal or concrete and is placed above the cooking zone. The purpose of the hood is to convey and disperse the fumes produced during cooking upwards.

How to maintain your gas outdoor griddle

A GUIDE FOR CLEANING AND STORAGE OUTDOOR GAS GRIDDLE

After using the grill, it is good practice to thoroughly clean all the elements used.

There are general guidelines to follow for cleaning the outdoor gas griddle.

First of all, never use the classic products you use for cleaning the kitchen or oven. This is because, in addition to being corrosive, they can leave residues that alter the taste of food.

If you do not have time to immediately clean the gas griddle after cooking, leave it on with the flame at minimum, and put a container full of water inside, so that the steam that is generated will keep the encrustations shaft until you are in order to clean it.

If the grids are not very large, after brushing them, you can put them to wash in the dishwasher. As soon as you have finished washing them, dry them well and apply a little grate oil.

If you have a steamer, you can use it to remove dirt, grease, and grate residues. As for the grids, just heat up as much as possible, so as to melt all the residual fat that is stuck. Then, always hot, remove the residues with pads or abrasive brushes, generally made with metal bristles. Spray some degreasing, cleaning products and finish cleaning the grill.

As for the cooking stones and plates, start by scraping the cooking surface, while they are still hot, with a spatula. As soon as they are cold, rub them with a steel wool and coarse salt. Rinse under running water and remember not to use my detergents or soaps.

As for the wooden trolley, it must be treated at least once a year, with wood oil and a special impregnating agent.

As for soap stones, for the first time you use them, clean the cooking surface well with a sponge and let it dry. Then sprinkle the surface with cooking oil, and let it absorb for a couple of hours. The next cleaning must be done when the stone is still warm. Scrape the surface with a spatula, sprinkle it with a little salt, and then dab it with a kitchen cloth or absorbent paper. Also in this case, avoid the use of soaps or detergents of any kind.

As for the inside of the lid and the side walls, clean them with the help of a silicone rather than a metal spatula, or a brazier scraper, in order to remove the carbon and grease deposits that accumulate, in order to particularly in the area of the lid.

For what about gas griddle storage follow these tips:

1. Remove the Propane Tank.

2. Clean well your outdoor Grill: you can use all tips we have given you above. The crucial element of cleaning a gas grill is to ensure it is not wet when moving to a storage unit.

3. Secure the Lid: If you have a gas grill that does not have a locking mechanism, place a piece of packing tape on the unit to secure the top lid. Fold up all other parts of the grill to make it easier to move.

4. Add a Waterproof Cover to your Grill: a cover offers added protection when storing a gas grill in a storage unit.

5. Store Upright: Your gas grill is designed to be stored and used in an upright position. Make sure that you have enough room in the moving truck and in your self-storage unit for the appliance to remain in its natural state.

HOW TO RECONDITION THE STONE AFTER A LONG STOP PERIOD

To have a perfect recondition it after a long stop period for your griddle, apply the same advice as for the first use. However, it would be better not to leave it unused for a long time.

However, from time to time, after having cleaned it thoroughly, repeat the treatment done before use: grease it, let it rest for a few hours, dry it well, removing excess grease and then store it waiting for the next use.

HOW TO SEASON A BLACKSTONE GRIDDLE

In this section of the book, I would like to tell you some other good tips about how to season a Blackstone griddle after a period of not use.

Seasoning is the process of burning oil into your cooktop. That oil will leave behind compounds which will create a hard surface on griddle.

First thing you have to do is fire up your griddle top and turn it high heat. After about 10 minutes you will start to see small spots appear on your griddle top.

Now grab a pair of rubber gloves, best is Blackstone gloves, so you do not get your hands all greasy.

For seasoning you can use any type of oil, such as vegetable oil, canola oil or olive oil. Instead, you can use Blackstone griddle seasoning to season your griddle top.

Put a pair of tablespoons of oil, or Blackstone seasoning, in a cloth and with the help of a pair of tongs or a spatula, go straight down onto the griddle top and rub this onto all the surface of the griddle.

Be sure to maintain the oil layer thin and smooth.

If you have too much oil or it seems uneven, use additional paper towel to wipe. The layer as smooth and even as is possible.

Allow the oil to eat up and smoke until the smoking has stopped. You should see griddle top start turn into various shades of yellow, then brown and finally again black.

The most important thing I want you to remember is to repeat the process 4 more times, reminding you to pass the oil even in the edges.

Cooking and temperature chart

Below you will find tables with times, temperatu¬re, and weight of the various foods to be grilled.

POULTRY	Weight/size	Method	Temperature	Duration	Medium	Well done
Whole chicken	42.3 oz	Indirect	356°F	50-60 min.		167°F
Chicken breast (with bone)	8 oz	Direct / Indirect	356°F	30-35 min.		167°F
Chicken breast (without bone)	8 oz	Direct	320°F	15-20 min.		167°F
Chicken leg	8 oz	Direct / Indirect	356°F	25–35 min.		167°F
Chicken wings	2.6 oz	Indirect	356°F	15-20 min.		167°F
Whole turkey	246.9 oz	Indirect	338°F	3–4 hours		176°F
Turkey breast, with bone	52.9 oz	Indirect	356°F	60–90 min.		176°F
Turkey breast (without bone)	52.9	Indirect	356°F	55–65 min.		176°F
Turkey leg	22.9 oz	Direct / Indirect	356°F	55–65 min.		176°F
Diced turkey breast (on skewers)	12.3 oz	Direct	356°F	12–15 min.		167°F
Whole duck	59.9 oz	Indirect	320°F	1,5 - 2 hours	122 - 131°F	149 - 158 °F
Duck breast fillet	7.7 oz	Direct / Indirect	356 - 392°F	10 - 15 min.		
Whole pheasant/guinea fowl	42.3 oz	Indirect	320 - 338°F	40 - 45 min.		
Whole goose	246.9 oz	Indirect	284- 302°F	3 - 4 hours		152 - 158°F
Chicken burgers	5.2 oz	Direct / Indirect	356 - 392°F	10 - 12 min.		166°F

BEEF/VEAL	Weight/size	Method	Temperature	Duration	Rare	Medium	Well done
Rump steak, fillet steak, T-bone steak	7 oz	Direct / Indirect	392 - 428°F	10 - 12 min.			
Ox steak	14 oz	Direct / Indirect		14 - 16 min.			
Beef roast from prime rib	88 oz	Indirect	284 - 302°F	1.5 - 2 hours			
Sirloin (without bone)	88 oz	Indirect	266°F	2 - 2.5 hours			
Brisket	88 oz	Indirect		2.5 - 3 hours			
Veal steak	7 oz	Direct / Indirect	356°F	10 - 12 min.		136 - 140°F	158 - 172°F
Veal steak	7 oz	Direct / Indirect	356°F	approx. 14 min.			
Veal steak	10.5 oz	Direct / Indirect	356°F	16 - 18 min.			
Hamburger	7 oz	Direct / Indirect	356 - 392°F	approx. 10 - 12 min.	125 - 131°F	136 - 140°F	155 - 158 °F

PORK	Weight/size	Method	Temperature	Duration	Medium	Well done
Chop	10.5 oz	Direct / Indirect		10 - 12 min.		149 - 154°F
Roast sirloin	70 oz	Indirect	302 - 320°F	1 - 1.5 hours	140 - 149°F	158 - 167°F
Spareribs	59.9 oz	Indirect	266°F	4 - 5 hours		
Pork fillet	15.8 oz	Direct / Indirect		25 - 35 min.	158 - 161°F	
Sausages, boiled	4.2 oz	Direct / Indirect		8 - 10 Min		
Sausages, boiled	3.5 oz	Direct / Indirect		8 - 10 min.		
Sausages, raw	4.2 oz	Direct / Indirect	180°F	15 - 20 min.	70 - 72°F	
Sausages, raw	3.5 oz	Direct / Indirect	180°F	10 - 15 min.	70 - 72°F	

LAMB	Weight/size	Method	Temperature	Duration	Medium	Well done
Chop	10.5 oz	Direct / Indirect	356°F	10 - 12 min.	131 - 136°F	158 - 161°F
Leg of lamb	59.9 oz	Indirect	284 - 320°F	55 - 65 min.	131 - 136°F	158 - 161°F
Leg of lamb from rolled roast	88 oz	Indirect	284- 320°F	15 - 20 min.	131 - 136°F	158- 161°F
Hock, deboned and flat	59.9 oz	Indirect		55 - 65 min.		
Hock, deboned as rolled roast	88 oz	Indirect		1,5 - 2 hours		
Rack of lamb	21 oz	Direct / Indirect		15 - 20 Min	131 - 136°F	158 - 161°F
Lamb ribs	52.9 oz	Indirect	284 - 302°F	75 - 90 min.		

Fish	Weight/size	Method	Temperature	Duration	Medium	Well done
Fish fillets (with skin)	6.3 oz	Direct (on the skin)	338°F	6 - 8 min.		149°F
Salmon steak	7 oz	Direct / Indirect	320°F	8 - 10 min.	122 - 140°F	149°F
Diced fish (on skewers)	10.5 oz	Indirect	356°F	10 - 12 min.		149°F
Whole fish	14 oz	Indirect	356°F	20 min.		140 - 149°F
Tuna steak	8.8 oz	Indirect	320 - 356°F	2 - 3 min.	122- 125°F	
Tuna steak	35 oz	Indirect	356°F	45 - 50 min.	122 - 125°F	

List of the main condiments
///
for the grill

Here are the spice mixes, the ones from which to start and that every self-respecting griller should know and master to always make its excellent grilled.

The purpose of the rub for the grill is to flavor and caramelize the meat thanks to the presence of sugar contained in the mixture.

Below you will find the list of the best rubs for seasoning meat and fish:

1. SPG Rub (Salt, Pepper, Garlic).
2. Rub SPOG (salt, pepper, onion, garlic).
3. Meathead Goldwyn's Memphis Dust Rub.
4. Classic Sweet Rub.
5. Steven Raichlen's Memphis Style Rub for Ribs.
6. Texas Style BBQ Rub.
7. Big Bad Beef Rub.
8. Magic Dust Rub.
9. Jack Daniel's Pork Rub.
10. Stubb's Bar-B-Q Chicken Spice Rub.
11. Rub Smokehouse BBQ.
12. Herb & Spice Rub Greek Lemon & Oregano.
13. Rub Caribbean Jerk.
14. Meat Church 'Holy Gospel' Seasoning.
15. Killer Hogs 'The BBQ Rub'.
16. Lane's BBQ Signature Rub.
17. Kosmos Q 'Cow Cover' Rub.
18. Traeger Winemaker's Napa Valley Rub.
19. Slap Yo Daddy BBQ 'Moola' Beef Rub.
20. Hardcore Carnivore 'Black' BBQ Rub.
21. Plowboys Yardbird Rub.
22. Lawry's Perfect Blend Chicken Rub.
23. Fords Gourmet Foods Bone Suckin' All Purpose Rub.
24. The Salt Lick Dry Rub.

Cinnamon griddle pancake

35 MINUTES

10 MINUTES

6

INGREDIENTS

- » 7 oz of flour
- » 2 eggs
- » 1.7 oz of sugar
- » 1 oz of butter
- » 1 cup of milk
- » 2 tsp of baking powder
- » 1 pinch of baking soda
- » 1 tablespoon of apple cider vinegar
- » 1 pinch of salt

For the stuffing
- » 1.7 oz of butter
- » 1 tsp of cinnamon powder
- » 3 tbsp of brown sugar

DIRECTIONS

1. Place the griddle on the grill and let it preheat to 375 ° F.
2. Put all the sifted dry ingredients in a bowl: flour, sugar, baking soda, salt and yeast.
3. Shell the eggs, divide the yolks from the whites and place them in two separate bowls.
4. Beat the egg whites until stiff.
5. Mix the egg yolks, milk, melted butter and vinegar.
6. At this point, combine the dry and liquid ingredients, mixing quickly with a whisk to avoid the formation of lumps.
7. Finally, add the egg whites and mix from bottom to top to prevent them from falling apart.
8. Prepare the filling now. Melt the butter in a double boiler and add the sugar and cinnamon. Mix well and place the mixture in a pastry bag.
9. When the griddle is hot, grease it with olive oil.
10. Pour ¼ of the batter over the griddle.
11. As soon as you see bubbles start to form on the surface, form a spiral with the cinnamon mixture.
12. Cook for a few more seconds, then turn your pancake with a sharp movement. Let it cook for 1 minute and remove it from the pan.
13. Proceed in this way for all pancakes until the batter is used up.
14. When all the pancakes are ready, divide them into plates, sprinkle with maple syrup and serve.

Classic griddles french toast

10 MINUTES

5 MINUTES

4

INGREDIENTS

» 12 slices of brioche bread
» 3 eggs
» ½ glass of milk
» 2.8 oz of butter
» Powdered sugar to taste
» Blueberries or other fruit to taste
» Honey to taste

DIRECTIONS

1. Place the griddle on the grill and preheat at 356 ° F for 10 minutes.
2. Shell the eggs in a bowl. Beat the eggs together with the milk using a fork.
3. Dip, one at a time, the slices of brioche bread on both sides, avoiding soaking them excessively.
4. Place the slices of bread on a plate next to each other.
5. When the griddle is hot enough, add the butter and let it melt.
6. Put the slices of bread and cook for 2 minutes per side.
7. Once cooked, dab the slices of bread with a paper towel and then place them on serving dishes.
8. Sprinkle the French toast with fruit and honey, sprinkle with icing sugar and serve.

Griddle breakfast potato pancakes

15 MINUTES

15 MINUTES

4

INGREDIENTS

» 3 boiled potatoes
» 1 onion
» 1 egg
» 1 tbsp of flour
» Olive oil to taste
» Salt and pepper to taste

DIRECTIONS

1. Place the griddle on the grill and preheat to 392 ° F for 10 minutes.
2. Peel the potatoes, cut them into small pieces and put them in the mixer.
3. Peel the onion, cut it into pieces and put it in the mixer with the potatoes.
4. on the mixer and purée everything.
5. At this point, transfer the mixture into a bowl, add the flour, egg, salt and pepper and mix the ingredients well.
6. When the griddle is ready, brush it with olive oil and spoon the mixture into it, trying to make discs as regular as possible.
7. Cook for 7 minutes on each side, then remove the pancakes from the plate.
8. Place the potato pancakes on serving plates and serve.

Grilled cheese and bacon omelette

10 MINUTES

12 MINUTES

4

INGREDIENTS

- » 4 whole eggs
- » 4 egg whites
- » 2.8 oz of cheddar
- » 2.8 oz of bacon
- » Salt and pepper to taste

DIRECTIONS

1. Preheat the grill to 356 ° F for 10 minutes.
2. Shell the eggs in a bowl, add salt and pepper and beat them with a fork.
3. In another bowl, put the egg whites and whisk them until stiff peaks are made.
4. Add the egg whites to the eggs and mix, from bottom to top, until they are completely incorporated.
5. When the plate is hot enough, add the bacon and cook 2 minutes per side.
6. Brush a pan with olive oil and pour the egg mixture inside.
7. Put the sliced cheddar and bacon slices on top and place the pan inside the grill.
8. Close the lid and cook for 12 minutes.
9. After cooking, remove the pan from the grill and let it rest for 5 minutes.
10. Cut the omelette into 4 parts, place them on serving plates and serve.

Griddle omelette with apple

15 MINUTES

24 MINUTES

4

INGREDIENTS

- » 4 eggs
- » 2 apples
- » 1.7 oz of sugar
- » 1 tsp of cinnamon powder
- » Powdered sugar to taste

DIRECTIONS

1. Preheat the grill to 356 ° F for 10 minutes.
2. Shell the eggs in a bowl and beat them with a fork.
3. Peel the apples, remove the seeds, and cut them into slices.
4. Place two cast iron pans on the grill and brush them with a little olive oil.
5. Put a little egg mixture in a pan and cook the first omelet for 3 minutes on each side and then switch to the other.
6. Repeat the same operation for all 4 omelets.
7. In the other pan, put the apples, sugar and cinnamon and cook until the sugar has completely dissolved.
8. When cooked, place the omelets on 4 serving plates.
9. Season the omelets with the caramelized apples, sprinkle the surface with a little powdered sugar, close them in half and serve.

TIPS: For a more complete breakfast, I recommend combining it with the Griddle Banana Bread recipe

Griddle pancakes stuffed with bacon and eggs

INGREDIENTS

- » 5 eggs
- » 4 tomatoes
- » 1 cup of whole milk
- » 4 slices of smoked bacon
- » Oz of canned sweet corn
- » 4.2 oz of yellow flour
- » 2.1 oz of flour
- » 2 tbsp of butter
- » ½ tsp of bicarbonate
- » ½ tsp of yeast
- » Olive oil to taste
- » Salt and pepper to taste

DIRECTIONS

1. Place the griddle on the grill and preheat to 375 ° F for 10 minutes.
2. Meanwhile, mix the yellow flour with the flour, a pinch of salt, baking powder, baking soda, 2 tablespoons of oil, milk and 1 egg.
3. Stir until you get a thick and smooth batter.
4. Brush the griddle with olive oil and put the batter on top.
5. Cook the pancakes until bubbles have formed; turn them and cook for another 30 seconds.
6. Continue until you have used up all the batter.
7. Wash and cut the tomatoes in half and cook them on the griddle about 1 minute on each side.
8. Put the bacon on the griddle and cook 3 minutes per side.
9. Now melt the butter on the griddle and then shell the eggs on top.
10. Mix the eggs and cook for 4 minutes, season with salt and pepper and put them on a plate.
11. Place the pancakes on the plates, stuff them with the eggs, grilled tomatoes, corn, and bacon and serve..

15 MINUTES

15 MINUTES

4

Griddle potato and onion omelette

20 MINUTES

30 MINUTES

4

INGREDIENTS

- » 21 oz of potatoes
- » 1.4 oz of grated Parmesancheese
- » 1 tbsp of chopped thyme
- » 3 eggs
- » 2 onions
- » Salt and pepper to taste
- » Olive oil to taste

DIRECTIONS

1. Preheat the grill to 356 ° F for 10 minutes.
2. Meanwhile, peel the potatoes, remove them, and then cut them into very thin slices.
3. Peel and wash the onions and then slice them.
4. When the grill is ready, put a cast iron pan on top and add 3 tablespoons of olive oil.
5. When the oil is hot, add the onions and fry for 5 minutes.
6. Now add the potatoes, season with salt and pepper, mix well and cook for 15 minutes.
7. Shell the eggs in a bowl and add the parmesan, thyme, salt, and pepper.
8. Beat the eggs with a fork until you get a homogeneous mixture.
9. Pour the egg mixture over the potatoes, cook for 8 minutes, and then turn the omelette.
10. Continue cooking for another 2 minutes and then remove the pan from the grill.
11. Divide the omelette into 4 parts, put it on serving plates and serve.

Griddle scrambled eggs with bacon and thyme

10 MINUTES

10 MINUTES

4

INGREDIENTS

- » 6 eggs
- » 12 slices of bacon
- » 2.1 oz of butter
- » 2 tbsp of milk
- » 2 tbsp of chopped thyme
- » Salt and pepper to taste
- » Olive oil to taste

DIRECTIONS

1. Preheat the grill to 356 ° F for 10 minutes.
2. Shell the eggs in a bowl, add the milk, thyme, salt, and pepper and beat them with a fork.
3. Brush a cast iron skillet with olive oil and heat it on the grill.
4. When the pan is hot, pour in the egg mixture, and cook for 6 minutes, stirring constantly.
5. When cooked, remove the pan from the grill and place the bacon slices.
6. Grill them for 2 minutes on each side and then remove them from the grill.
7. Divide the eggs into serving plates, add the bacon and serve.

Griddle scrambled eggs with cheddar

10 MINUTES

6 MINUTES

4

INGREDIENTS

- » 5 eggs
- » 2.8 oz of cheddar
- » Salt and pepper to taste
- » Butter to taste

DIRECTIONS

1. Preheat the grill to 356 ° F for 10 minutes.
2. Shell the eggs in a bowl, add salt and pepper and beat them vigorously with a fork.
3. Put the butter in a cast iron skillet and then put the pan on the grill.
4. When the butter has melted, add the eggs.
5. Cook for 2 minutes, stirring constantly and then add the chopped cheddar.
6. Cook for another 4 minutes, always stirring.
7. After cooking, remove the pan from the grill.
8. Divide the scrambled eggs into 4 plates and serve.
9. Preheat the grill to 356 ° F for 10 minutes.
10. Shell the eggs in a bowl, add salt and pepper and beat them vigorously with a fork.
11. Put the butter in a cast iron skillet and then put the pan on the grill.
12. When the butter has melted, add the eggs.
13. Cook for 2 minutes, stirring constantly and then add the chopped cheddar.
14. Cook for another 4 minutes, always stirring.
15. After cooking, remove the pan from the grill.
16. Divide the scrambled eggs into 4 plates and serve.

Griddle tomato omelette

INGREDIENTS

- » 4 eggs
- » 2 tbsp of milk
- » 7 oz of cream cheese
- » 10.5 oz of cherry tomatoes
- » 4 basil leaves, chopped
- » Salt and pepper to taste
- » Olive oil to taste

DIRECTIONS

1. Place the griddle on the grill and preheat to 356 °F for 10 minutes.
2. Shell the eggs in a bowl, add the milk, salt and pepper and beat them with a fork.
3. When the plate is hot enough, add a little egg mixture and cook for 3 minutes per side.
4. Repeat the same operation for the other 3 omelets.
5. Once cooked, place the omelets on four serving plates.
6. Wash and dry the cherry tomatoes and then cut them into cubes.
7. Spread the surface of the omelets with the cream cheese, add the cherry tomatoes and basil leaves.
8. Season with a little salt and pepper, close the omelette and serve.

15 MINUTES

24 MINUTES

4

Griddle leek quiche

20 MINUTES

50 MINUTES

4

INGREDIENTS

» 1 roll of shortcrust pastry
» 2 tbsp of butter
» 10.5 oz of leeks
» 1 sprig of thyme
» 2 eggs
» 1 cup of cooking cream
» Salt and pepper to taste

DIRECTIONS

1. Preheat the grill to 374° F.
2. wash the leeks and cut them into rings.
3. Wash and dry the thyme and then chop the leaves.
4. When the grill is hot, put in a cast iron pan and melt the butter.
5. Add the leeks, season with salt and pepper and brown for 10 minutes.
6. Remove the pan from the grill and set aside.
7. Put the shelled eggs in a bowl and beat them with a fork.
8. Add the cooking cream and mix well.
9. Brush a tart mold and put the shortcrust pastry inside.
10. Pour the leeks into the pasta and then add the egg mixture.
11. Place the mold on the grill, close the lid and cook for 35 minutes.
12. After cooking, remove the mold from the grill and let it cool.
13. Then cut the quiche into slices, put them on plates and serve.

TIPS: I recommend that you combine this recipe with the Hibachi griddle chicken recipe

Griddle Margherita pizza

30 MINUTES
+ 15 HOURS
REST TIME

30 MINUTES

4 PIZZAS

INGREDIENTS

- » 10.5 oz of flour 0
- » 1 glass of water
- » 1 tsp of brewer's yeast
- » 7 oz of peeled tomatoes
- » 2 mozzarellas
- » 1 tsp of brown sugar
- » 4 fresh basil leaves
- » Olive oil to taste
- » Salt to taste

DIRECTIONS

1. Sift the flour on the work surface, arrange it in a heap and add the yeast, brown sugar and water.
2. Knead until you get a homogeneous and lump-free mixture.
3. Add the salt and knead again for a couple of minutes.
4. Shape it into a ball and place it in a container, cover it and let it rise in a warm place for 12 hours.
5. After 12 hours, resume the dough and knead again.
6. Divide the dough into four loaves of the same weight and then knead them with your hands to form 4 balls.
7. Put the loaves in a baking pan, cover and let rise for another 2 hours.
8. After the 2 hours, preheat the grill to 482 ° F.
9. Put the loaves on a floured surface and roll them out.
10. When the grill has reached temperature, place the pizza stone, and let it heat for 10 minutes.
11. Spread the peeled tomatoes on the pizzas and season with oil and salt.
12. Add the sliced mozzarella and basil leaves.
13. After 10 minutes, put the pizzas on the stone, close the lid and cook for 30 minutes.
14. After cooking, remove the pizza from the grill, cut it into 4 slices and serve.

Griddle pea and zucchini plumcake

20 MINUTES

40 MINUTES

4

INGREDIENTS

- » 14 oz of peas
- » 7 oz of Swiss cheese
- » 6.3 oz of flour
- » 2.8 oz of grated parmesan cheese
- » 3 eggs
- » 2 zucchinis
- » ½ glass of milk
- » 2 tsp of baking powder
- » ½ glass of extra virgin olive oil
- » Salt and pepper to taste

DIRECTIONS

1. Preheat the grill to 356 ° F.
2. Wash the peas and then let them drain.
3. Wash the zucchinis and then grate them in a bowl.
4. Put the eggs on a plate with the milk and beat them with a fork.
5. Sift the flour into a bowl with the baking powder and stir in the beaten eggs.
6. Mix well and then add the Parmesan, olive oil, salt, and pepper.
7. Stir until you get a homogeneous and lump-free mixture.
8. Add the zucchinis and peas, mix thoroughly with a wooden spoon until the mixture is as homogeneous as possible.
9. Cut the Swiss cheese into cubes, put it in the bowl with the dough and mix again.
10. Transfer the dough to a loaf pan and place the mold on the grill.
11. Close the lid and cook for 40 minutes.
12. After cooking, remove the mold from the grill and let it cool for 10 minutes.
13. Remove the plum cake from the mold, put it on a serving dish, cut it into slices and serve.

TIPS: For a full lunch or dinner I recommend combining this recipe with Chicken griddle kebab

Griddle pizza with olives, pepperoni, and capers

20 MINUTES

25 MINUTES

4

INGREDIENTS

- » 14 oz of cherry tomatoes
- » 30 oz of pizza dough
- » 4.2 oz of black olives
- » 7 oz of mozzarella
- » 3.5 oz of spicy salami
- » 2 tbsp of capers
- » Salt and pepper to taste
- » Olive oil to taste

DIRECTIONS

1. Preheat the grill to 482 ° F.
2. Divide the pizza dough into 4 loaves and then roll them out to form circles of the same size.
3. Wash and dry the cherry tomatoes and then cut them in half.
4. Rinse the capers under running water and then squeeze them.
5. Season the pizzas with a drizzle of oil and then spread the sliced mozzarella on top.
6. Add the capers, cherry tomatoes, olives, and spicy salami.
7. Season with a drizzle of oil, salt, and pepper.
8. When the grill has reached temperature, place the pizza stone, and heat it for 10 minutes.
9. After 10 minutes, put the pizzas on the stone, close the lid and cook for 25 minutes.
10. After cooking, remove the pizzas from the grill, cut them into 4 slices and serve.

Griddle quiche with smoked salmon

15 MINUTES

45 MINUTES

4

INGREDIENTS

» 1 roll of shortcrust pastry
» 5.2 oz of Gruyere
» 4 eggs
» 3 slices of smoked salmon
» 1 cup of cooking cream
» Salt and pepper to taste

DIRECTIONS

1. Preheat the grill to 356 ° F.
2. Take a tart mold, brush with olive oil and line with the shortcrust pastry.
3. Put the eggs and cream in a bowl, add salt and pepper and the grated Gruyere cheese and beat them with a fork until you get a homogeneous mixture.
4. Pour the egg mixture into the shortcrust pastry.
5. Add the slices of smoked salmon cut into small pieces and place the pan on the grill.
6. Close the lid and cook for 45 minutes.
7. After cooking, remove the mold from the grill and let it cool.
8. Then cut the quiche into 4 parts, put it on serving plates and serve.

TIPS: I recommend that you combine this recipe with Griddle Sea bream with lime and coriander

Beef and pork griddle burger with cheddar and bacon

20 MINUTES

15 MINUTES

4

INGREDIENTS

- » 9.8 oz of ground beef
- » 9.8 oz of minced pork
- » 1 onion
- » 4 slices of cheddar
- » 8 slices of bacon
- » 4 lettuce leaves
- » 4 hamburger buns
- » Ketchup to taste
- » Mayonnaise to taste

DIRECTIONS

1. Place the griddle on the grill and let it preheat at 356 ° F for 10 minutes.
2. Peel, wash and chop the onion.
3. Wash and dry the lettuce leaves and then cut them in half.
4. Put the pork and beef in a bowl.
5. Add the onion, salt and pepper and mix well.
6. Form 4 meatballs with the dough and then mash them lightly and finish the edges with a knife or a pastry ring.
7. When the plate is hot, place the burgers and cook them for 4 minutes per side.
8. Once cooked, remove the burgers, and add the bacon.
9. Cook for 2 minutes on each side and then remove from the grill.
10. Cut the buns in half and toast them for a couple of minutes.
11. Put the buns on the plates and put the lettuce on top.
12. Then put the hamburger, bacon and finally the cheddar.
13. Sprinkle with ketchup and mayonnaise, close the buns and serve.

Classic griddle smashed beef burger

PREPARATION: 15 MINUTES
COOKING: 6 MINUTES
PORTIONS: 4

INGREDIENTS

» 4 hamburger buns
» 10.5 oz of ground beef
» 4 lettuce leaves
» 2 red tomatoes
» 1 red onion
» 1 cucumber
» 1.4 oz of ketchup

DIRECTIONS

1. Place the griddle on the grill and let it preheat at 356 ° F for 10 minutes.
2. Meanwhile, put the beef in a bowl and add salt and pepper.
3. Mix well and then form 8 meatballs.
4. When the griddle is hot, put the meatballs on top.
5. Now mash the meatballs so that you have 4 burgers of the same size as the sandwich.
6. After 30 seconds, scrape the burgers and turn them upside down.
7. Cook for another 60 seconds, or until the core temperature of the meat has reached 149 ° F.
8. As soon as the smash burgers are cooked, remove them from the grill and let them rest.
9. Meanwhile, cut the buns in half and brush them with olive oil.
10. Put on the plate and toast them for 2 minutes.
11. Put the buns on the serving plates.
12. Wash and dry the lettuce leaves and place them on top of half of the rolls.
13. Wash the onion and tomatoes and then cut them into thin slices.
14. Put 1 smash burger on each bun.
15. Add the tomato and lettuce and top with the other half of the smash burger.
16. Sprinkle with ketchup, close with the other half of the sandwich and serve.

Griddle beef burger with parmesan

INGREDIENTS

- » 14 oz of minced beef
- » 2.8 oz of grated parmesancheese
- » 2 tomatoes
- » 4 hamburger buns
- » 4 lettuce leaves to taste
- » Bbq sauce to taste
- » Salt and pepper to taste
- » Balsamic vinegar to taste

DIRECTIONS

1. Place the griddle on the grill and let it preheat at 356 ° F for 10 minutes.
2. Meanwhile, put the meat in a bowl and add salt, pepper, and parmesan.
3. Stir until you get a homogeneous mixture.
4. With the help of a pastry cutter, form hamburgers that have, possibly, the same diameter as the buns.
5. When the griddle is hot, place the burgers on top and cook for 4 minutes per side.
6. Meanwhile, wash and dry the lettuce and tomatoes.
7. Then take the tomatoes and cut them into thin slices.
8. Once cooked, remove the burgers from the griddle and place the buns cut in half.
9. Toast the buns for 2 minutes, then remove them and put them on the plates.
10. Put the lettuce first and then the tomatoes on the bottom of the buns.
11. Place the burger on top, sprinkle with the bbq sauce, close the buns and serve.

15 MINUTES

10 MINUTES

4

Griddle hamburger with cheese sauce and mushrooms

20 MINUTES

12 MINUTES

4

INGREDIENTS

» 9.8 oz of ground beef
» 9.8 oz of minced pork
» 5.2 oz of Swiss cheese
» 3.5 oz of Champignon mushrooms
» 1 glass of cooking cream
» 4 hamburger buns
» Salt and pepper to taste

DIRECTIONS

1. Place the griddle on the grill and let it preheat at 356 ° F for 10 minutes.
2. In the meantime, remove the final part of the mushrooms, wash them, dry them and then cut them into small pieces.
3. Put the beef and pork in a bowl and season with salt and pepper.
4. Stir until you get a homogeneous mixture.
5. Form 4 meatballs with the dough and place them on a plate.
6. Squeeze them lightly and then round the edges.
7. Put the mushrooms, cheese and cream in a cast iron saucepan.
8. When the plate is hot, put the casserole and the hamburgers to cook.
9. Cook the burgers for 4 minutes on each side and, as they cook, stir the sauce continuously, until the cheese has completely melted.
10. Once cooked, remove the burgers and casserole from the grill.
11. Cut the buns in half, place them on the griddle and toast them for a couple of minutes.
12. Now put the buns on the plates.
13. Place the hamburger on top of the buns and sprinkle them with the mushroom and cheese sauce.
14. Close the buns and serve.

Griddle hamburger with eggs, Swiss and shallots

INGREDIENTS

- » 17.6 oz of ground beef
- » 1 shallot
- » 4 eggs
- » 2.8 oz of Swiss cheese
- » 1 onion
- » 4 hamburger buns
- » Salt and pepper to taste

DIRECTIONS

1. Place the griddle on the grill and let it preheat at 356 ° F for 10 minutes.
2. Peel, wash and chop the shallot and put it in a bowl.
3. Add the beef, salt and pepper and mix well.
4. With the help of a pastry cutter, form hamburgers that possibly have the same diameter as the sandwiches.
5. Peel and wash the onion and then cut it into thin slices.
6. Put the onion in a cast iron pan brushed with olive oil.
7. When the griddle is hot, put the pan on top and cook the onion for 3 minutes.
8. Put the shelled eggs on top of the onion and cook for another 5 minutes.
9. In the meantime, put the hamburgers on the griddle and cook for 3 minutes and then turn them.
10. Add the Swiss cheese on top of the burgers and cook for another 3 minutes.
11. Once cooked, remove the pan and the hamburgers from the griddle.
12. Cut the buns in half and toast them on the griddle for a couple of minutes.
13. When the buns are ready, remove them from the plate and place them on the plates.
14. Place the burger on top of the buns and then place the onion eggs on top.
15. Place the other half of the bun next to it and serve.

15 MINUTES

15 MINUTES

4

Pork burger griddle with pumpkin and cheese

PREPARATION: 15 MINUTES
COOKING: 15 MINUTES
PORTIONS: 4

INGREDIENTS

» 4 classic hamburger buns
» 14 oz of ground pork
» 7 oz of pumpkin pulp
» 1 tsp of fennel seeds
» 1 pinch of nutmeg
» 4.2 oz of fresh spreadable cheese
» 1.4 oz of bbq sauce
» Olive oil to taste
» Salt and pepper to taste

DIRECTIONS

1. Preheat the grill to 356 ° F for 10 minutes.
2. Meanwhile, wash and dry the pumpkin pulp and then cut it into thin slices.
3. Put the meat in a bowl and season with salt, pepper, fennel seeds and nutmeg.
4. Stir until you get a homogeneous mixture.
5. Form four meatballs with the meat and then flatten them slightly and trim the edges with a knife.
6. When the grill is hot, put the pumpkin and cook it for 4 minutes per side.
7. When it is cooked, remove it and put it on a plate. Season with oil, salt and pepper and set aside.
8. Place the plate on the grill and let it heat for 10 minutes.
9. When the griddle is hot, put the burgers on.
10. Cook for 4 minutes and then turn them.
11. Cook for another 4 minutes.
12. Meanwhile, cut the buns in half and brush them with olive oil.
13. Put them on the plate and toast them for 2 minutes.
14. When the buns and burgers are cooked, remove them from the grill and place them on the plates.
15. Put on half the sandwich, first the pumpkin, then the cheese and finally the hamburger.
16. Sprinkle with the bbq sauce, close the buns and serve.

Salmon griddle burger with flavored mayonnaise

25 MINUTES

8 MINUTES

4

INGREDIENTS

» 4 hamburger buns
» 21 oz of salmon fillet
» 10.5 oz of mayonnaise
» 2 cloves of garlic
» 1 tbsp of chopped dill
» 4 pickled gherkins
» 1 tbsp of chopped chives
» 2 large tomatoes
» 4 lettuce leaves
» Salt and pepper to taste

DIRECTIONS

1. Start by preparing the flavored mayonnaise.
2. Put the mayonnaise in a bowl and add the dill and the peeled and chopped garlic cloves.
3. Mix well and put in the fridge.
4. Place the griddle on the grill and let it preheat at 356 ° F for 10 minutes.
5. Meanwhile, wash the salmon, remove the skin and bones and then chop it with a knife.
6. Put the salmon in a bowl and add salt, pepper and chives.
7. Stir until you get a homogeneous mixture.
8. With the help of a pastry cutter, form hamburgers that have, possibly, the same diameter as the buns.
9. When the griddle is hot enough, add the burgers and cook for 3 minutes per side.
10. When cooked, remove the burgers, and put the buns cut in half.
11. Toast them for a couple of minutes, then remove them from the griddle and put them on the plates.
12. Wash and dry the tomatoes and lettuce, then cut the tomatoes into slices.
13. Spread some mayonnaise on the bottom of the buns.
14. Put the lettuce and tomatoes on top and finally the hamburger.
15. Sprinkle with the rest of the mayonnaise, close the buns and serve.

Smashed griddle pork and beef burger with curry

15 MINUTES

10 MINUTES

4

INGREDIENTS

- » 9.8 oz of ground beef
- » 9.8 oz of minced pork
- » 1 tbsp of curry powder
- » 4 slices of Swiss cheese
- » 4 tbsp of bbq sauce
- » 4 hamburger buns
- » 4 pickled peppers
- » Salt and pepper to taste

DIRECTIONS

1. Place the griddle on the grill and let it preheat at 356 ° F for 10 minutes.
2. Put the pork and beef in a bowl.
3. Add the curry powder, salt and pepper and mix well.
4. Form 8 meatballs and, when the plate is hot, put them to cook.
5. Mash the meatballs as much as possible and cook for 1 minute.
6. Turn them over and put the cheese on top.
7. Cook for 1 minute and then close with the other half of the meatballs.
8. Cook for 2 minutes and then remove them from the griddle.
9. Cut the buns in half, place them on the griddle and toast them for 2 minutes.
10. Put the buns on the plates. Place the pickled peppers on the bottom and the smashed burger on top.
11. Sprinkle with the bbq sauce, close the buns and serve.

Smashed lime marinated griddle turkey burger

INGREDIENTS

- » 35.2 oz of minced turkey meat
- » 4 hamburger buns
- » 4 slices of Cheddar
- » 2 limes
- » 1 clove of garlic
- » 1 tablespoon of cornstarch
- » Salt and pepper to taste
- » Olive oil to taste

DIRECTIONS

1. Place the griddle on the grill and let it preheat at 356 ° F for 10 minutes.
2. Wash and dry the limes, grate the zest and strain the juice into a bowl.
3. Peel, wash and chop the garlic and place it in the bowl with the limes.
4. Add 4 tablespoons of oil, salt and pepper and mix well.
5. Now add the turkey meat and mix until you get a homogeneous mixture.
6. Add the cornstarch and mix well, then form 8 meatballs with the dough.
7. When the plate is hot, put the meatballs on top.
8. Mash the meatballs and cook for 3 minutes.
9. Turn the meatballs and cook for another 2 minutes.
10. Add the Cheddar and put another meatball on top of the cheese.
11. Cook for another 2 minutes.
12. Meanwhile, cut the buns in half and brush them with olive oil.
13. Put the buns on the griddle and toast them for 2 minutes.
14. Once cooked, remove the buns and hamburger from the griddle.
15. Put the burger on half of the bun, sprinkle with the ketchup and then close with the other half of the bun and serve.

15 MINUTES

8 MINUTES

4

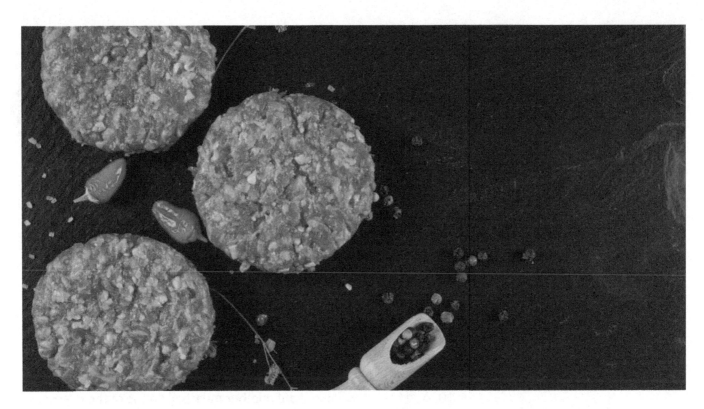

Smashed pork and chicken griddle burger with crispy bacon

PREPARATION: 20 MINUTES
COOKING: 10 MINUTES
PORTIONS: 4

INGREDIENTS

- » 14 oz of ground chicken meat
- » 5.6 oz of ground pork
- » 1 onion
- » 4 slices of bacon
- » 4 hamburger buns
- » 4 lettuce leaves
- » 4 tbsp of bbq sauce
- » Salt and pepper to taste

DIRECTIONS

1. Place the griddle on the grill and let it preheat at 356° F for 10 minutes.
2. Peel, wash and chop the onion.
3. Wash and dry the lettuce leaves.
4. Put the chicken and pork in a bowl.
5. Add salt, pepper, and the chopped onion.
6. Using a fork, gently mix the mixture and then form 8 meatballs.
7. When the plate is hot, put the meatballs on top.
8. Mash the meatballs and cook for 3 minutes, then turn them and continue for another 3 minutes.
9. Remove the smashed burgers from the plate and place the bacon and buns cut in half on top.
10. Toast the buns for 2 minutes and then remove them from the griddle.
11. Cook the bacon for 2 minutes on each side and then remove it from the griddle.
12. Put the buns on the plates. Place a lettuce leaf on top of each bun and then half of the hamburger.
13. Put the bacon on top of the burger and then add the other half of the burger.
14. Sprinkle with the bbq sauce, close the buns and serve.

Griddle BLT sandwich

15 MINUTES

10 MINUTES

4

INGREDIENTS

» 8 slices of toast bread
» 8 slices of tomato
» 12 slices of bacon
» A few lettuces leave
» 4 tsp of mayonnaise

DIRECTIONS

1. Preheat the grill to 356 ° F for 10 minutes.
2. When the grill is hot enough, add the bacon and brown it for 3 minutes on each side.
3. Remove the bacon and put the bread. Toast for 2 minutes on each side, then remove from the grill and place on plates.
4. Spread the mayonnaise on the bread, add the lettuce and tomatoes and finally put the bacon.
5. Close with the other slice of bread, lightly press the sandwich with your fingertips and serve.

Griddle Club sandwich

PREPARATION: 20 MINUTES
COOKING: 10 MINUTES
PORTIONS: 4

INGREDIENTS

- » 17.6 oz of thinly sliced turkey breast
- » 24 slices of bacon
- » 6 tomatoes
- » 20 lettuce leaves
- » 7 oz of mayonnaise
- » 12 slices of crustless toast bread

DIRECTIONS

1. Preheat the grill to 356 ° F for 10 minutes.
2. Wash and dry the turkey slices, brush with oil and season with salt and pepper.
3. Wash and dry the tomatoes and then cut them into thin slices.
4. Wash the lettuce leaves, dab them with a kitchen towel and then cut them into pieces that are not too small.
5. When the grill is hot enough, put the turkey in and cook for 5 minutes per side.
6. Remove the turkey and add the bacon. Cook for 2 minutes on each side and then remove from the grill.
7. Now put the slices of bread. Toast it for two minutes on each side and then remove it from the grill and place it on a cutting board.
8. Start composing the sandwiches. Spread the mayonnaise on a slice of bread.
9. Place some lettuce and turkey on top.
10. Arrange the tomato and bacon on top. Top with a slice of bread, repeat the inner layers with mayonnaise, lettuce, turkey, tomato, and smoked bacon. Close with the third slice of bread and then cut the sandwich in half.
11. Proceed in the same way for the other sandwiches.
12. As soon as you have finished putting all the sandwiches together, put them on serving plates and serve.

Griddle sandwiches stuffed with chicken

20 MINUTES

20 MINUTES

4

INGREDIENTS

- » 8 slices of toast bread
- » 14 oz of chicken breast
- » 3.5 oz of fresh spreadable cheese
- » 1.7 oz of bean sprouts
- » 2 tomatoes
- » A few lettuces leave
- » 1 tbsp of mustard
- » Chopped thyme, sage, and rosemary to taste
- » Salt and pepper to taste
- » Olive oil to taste

DIRECTIONS

1. Preheat the grill to 392 ° F for 10 minutes.
2. Wash and dry the tomatoes, cut them into slices and set aside.
3. Wash and dry the lettuce leaves.
4. Wash and dry the chicken breast, cut it in half and brush it with olive oil.
5. Sprinkle the surface of the meat with the chopped aromatic herbs, salt, and pepper.
6. When the grill is hot enough, place the chicken and cook for 8 minutes per side.
7. Once cooked, remove the chicken, and put the bread to toast.
8. Cook for 2 minutes on each side, then remove it from the grill and put it on plates.
9. Place the chicken on a cutting board and cut it into slices
10. Brush the surface of the sandwich with the cream cheese and then place the bean sprouts on top.
11. Spread the chicken slices over the bean sprouts and place the tomatoes, lettuce leaves and a little mustard on top.
12. Close with the other slice of sandwich and serve.

Griddle sandwich with chicken and avocado

10 MINUTES

15 MINUTES

4

INGREDIENTS

» 9.8 oz thinly sliced chicken breast.
» 12 slices of toast bread
» 2 avocados
» 4 tbsp of mayonnaise
» 20 cherry tomatoes
» Salt and pepper to taste
» Olive oil to taste

DIRECTIONS

1. Preheat the grill to 392 ° F for 10 minutes.
2. Meanwhile, brush the chicken with olive oil and season with salt and pepper.
3. When the grill is hot enough, place the chicken slices and cook them for 4 minutes per side.
4. When the chicken is ready, remove it from the grill and put the slices of bread to toast for two minutes on each side.
5. Wash and dry the cherry tomatoes and then cut them into thin slices.
6. Peel the avocado, remove the stones, and cut the pulp into slices.
7. Put the slices of bread on the plates and spread some mayonnaise.
8. Place a slice of grilled chicken breast and a couple of slices of avocado on top.
9. Place the cherry tomatoes on top of the avocado slices, cover with a slice of bread, which you will season in the same way: mayonnaise, chicken, avocado, cherry tomatoes and close with another slice of bread.
10. Repeat the same procedure for the other sandwiches and then serve.

Griddle sandwich with crispy bacon and mustard

15 MINUTES

10 MINUTES

4

INGREDIENTS

- » 4 sandwiches
- » 14.1 oz of bacon cut into thin slices
- » 4 ripe red tomatoes
- » 8 tbsp of mayonnaise
- » 6 tbsp of mustard with grains
- » 8 lettuce leaves

DIRECTIONS

1. Preheat the grill to 356 °F for 10 minutes.
2. Meanwhile, wash and dry the tomatoes and then cut them into thin slices.
3. Wash and dry the lettuce leaves.
4. When the grill is hot, oil it well and then put the bacon on top.
5. Cook for 3 minutes on each side, then remove from the grill and place on plates.
6. Cut the sandwiches in half, brush them with olive oil and toast them for 1 minute per side.
7. Remove the sandwiches from the grill and place them on the plates.
8. Spread the mayonnaise on the surface of the sandwiches, then put the lettuce, tomatoes and finally the bacon on top.
9. Sprinkle the surface of the bacon with mustard, close the sandwiches and serve.

Griddle sandwiches with lamb ragout and yogurt

PREPARATION: 20 MINUTES
COOKING: 2 H 20 MINUTES
PORTIONS: 4

INGREDIENTS

- » 4 sandwiches
- » 28.2 oz of ground lamb
- » 8.8 oz of Greek yogurt
- » 4 lettuce leaves
- » 1 tbsp of saffron
- » 1 glass of white wine
- » 1 tsp of chopped chives
- » 1 tsp of garlic powder
- » 1 tsp of minced mint
- » 1 tsp of cumin powder
- » 1 tsp of chopped parsley
- » 1 tbsp of concentrated tomato
- » Salt and pepper to taste
- » Olive oil to taste

DIRECTIONS

1. Pass the hour, take the lamb out of the fridge, and preheat the grill to 356 ° F for 10 minutes.
2. When the grill is ready, put a cast iron saucepan and let it heat up.
3. When the saucepan is hot enough, heat two tablespoons of olive oil.
4. Add the lamb meat and brown it for 5 minutes.
5. Add the white wine and let it evaporate.
6. Add the tomato, chives, garlic, mint, cumin, saffron and parsley.
7. Mix well, season with salt and pepper and a glass of hot water.
8. Cover the saucepan, switch to indirect cooking, and cook the sauce for 2 hours, stirring occasionally and adding a little water, if needed.
9. After cooking, remove the saucepan from the grill and let it rest.
10. Wash and dry the lettuce leaves and divide them in half.
11. Put the yogurt in a bowl, season it with oil, salt and pepper and mix well.
12. Open the sandwiches in half and place them on the plates.
13. Place the lettuce leaves and then the lamb ragout inside the sandwiches.
14. Sprinkle with the yogurt sauce, close the sandwiches and serve.

Griddle sandwich with pumpkin and sausage

INGREDIENTS

- » 4 sandwiches
- » 17.1 oz of pumpkin pulp
- » 7 oz of pork sausage
- » 4.2 oz of Parmesan
- » 2 sprigs of rosemary
- » Balsamic vinegar to taste
- » Salt and pepper to taste
- » Olive oil to taste

DIRECTIONS

1. Preheat the grill to 392 ° F for 10 minutes and set it up for indirect cooking.
2. Wash and dry the pumpkin pulp and then cut it into cubes.
3. Wash and dry the rosemary.
4. Brush a baking pan with olive oil and put the pumpkin inside.
5. Add the rosemary, season with oil, salt and pepper and put the baking pan on the grill.
6. Close the lid and cook for 40 minutes.
7. After cooking, remove the baking pan from the grill, and let the pumpkin cool.
8. Oil the grill and place the sausage in the center.
9. Turn it often, so that it takes on an even color.
10. Cook for 15 minutes and then check the cooking by cutting one end. If it is still raw, leave it on the grill for a few minutes.
11. Meanwhile, put the pumpkin in a bowl and mash it with a fork.
12. After cooking, remove the sausage from the grill, put it on a cutting board and cut it into 4 pieces.
13. Brush the rolls with olive oil and toast them for 1 minute per side.
14. Put the sandwiches on the plates. Spread the pumpkin on top, sprinkle the bottom with sausage and parmesan flakes and then sprinkle a little balsamic vinegar.
15. Close the sandwiches and serve.

20 MINUTES

50 MINUTES

4

Griddle sandwiches with strips of beef

PREPARATION: 20 MINUTES
COOKING: 15 MINUTES
PORTIONS: 4

INGREDIENTS

- » 4 sandwiches
- » 4 tbsp of mustard
- » 1 shallot
- » 3.5 oz of speck
- » ½ zucchini
- » 7 oz of beef rump
- » 1 tbsp of chopped rosemary
- » Salt and pepper to taste
- » Olive oil to taste

DIRECTIONS

1. Preheat the grill to 356 ° F for 10 minutes.
2. Brush the meat with olive oil and season with salt, pepper and rosemary.
3. When the grill is hot enough, put the meat on and grill it for 3 minutes on each side.
4. Meanwhile, wash the zucchini, cut it into thin slices and grill it for 1 minute per side.
5. Once the meat and zucchini are cooked, remove them from the grill and put the speck on.
6. Grill for 2 minutes on each side.
7. Meanwhile, peel and wash the shallot and then cut it into thin slices.
8. When all the ingredients are ready, you can start putting the sandwiches together.
9. Cut the sandwiches in half, put them on the serving plates and sprinkle them with mustard.
10. Cut the beef into small pieces and place it inside the sandwiches.
11. Add the zucchini, the shallot and finally the speck.
12. Close the sandwiches and serve.

Griddle sandwich with tofu, capers, and olives

15 MINUTES

10 MINUTES

4

INGREDIENTS

- » 8.8 oz of natural tofu
- » ½ shallot
- » 1 oz of black olives
- » 1 tbsp of capers
- » 3 tbsp of mustard
- » 4 tomatoes
- » 4 sandwiches
- » Olive oil to taste
- » Salt and pepper to taste

DIRECTIONS

1. Preheat the grill to 392 ° F for 10 minutes.
2. Dab the tofu with a paper towel and when the grill is hot, put it to grill.
3. Cook for 3 minutes on each side and then remove it from the grill and put it in a bowl.
4. Divide the sandwiches in half, brush them with olive oil and toast them for 2 minutes per side.
5. Remove the sandwiches from the grill and place them on the plates.
6. Add to the bowl with the tofu, oil, salt, pepper, olives, shallots, mustard, and capers.
7. Take an immersion blender and blend until you get a creamy and homogeneous mixture.
8. Wash the tomatoes and then cut them into slices.
9. Spread the tofu cream on the sandwiches, then put the tomato slices on top, close with the other half of the sandwich and serve.

Griddle sloppy joe

15 MINUTES

35 MINUTES

4

INGREDIENTS

- » 4 sandwiches
- » 17.6 oz of ground beef
- » 6 pieces of jalapeño
- » ½ onion
- » 1 pinch of cumin powder
- » A few drops of Worcestershire sauce
- » 7 oz of ketchup
- » 2 tsp of brown sugar
- » 1 clove of garlic
- » Olive oil to taste
- » 1 glass of water
- » Salt and pepper to taste

DIRECTIONS

1. Preheat the grill to 356 ° F for 10 minutes.
2. Meanwhile, peel the onion and then chop it.
3. When the grill is hot, put a cast iron saucepan on top and let it heat up.
4. Put 3 tablespoons of olive oil, let it heat up and then add the onion.
5. Cook for 2 minutes and then add the meat.
6. Mix well, cook for 5 minutes, and then add the jalapeno, cumin, garlic, ketchup, Worcestershire and brown sugar.
7. Mix well, then season with salt and pepper, add the water and put the lid on the saucepan.
8. Switch to indirect cooking and cook for 20 minutes, stirring occasionally.
9. After cooking, remove the saucepan from the grill and let it rest for 5 minutes.
10. Cut the sandwiches in half and place them on serving plates.
11. Fill the inside of the sandwiches with the meat, close them and serve.

Brandy Roast Griddle Chicken

INGREDIENTS

15 MINUTES

70 MINUTES

5

» 42.3 oz of whole chicken
» 1 clove garlic
» 2 bay leaves
» 1 glass of brandy
» 2 tbsp of melted butter
» 1 sprig of thyme
» ½ glass of white wine
» 1 sprig of rosemary
» Salt and pepper to taste

DIRECTIONS

1. Preheat the grill to 374 ° F for 10 minutes.
2. Meanwhile, wash and dry the bay leaves, rosemary, and thyme.
3. Peel and chop the garlic.
4. Salt and pepper the chicken inside and out and insert rosemary, garlic, bay leaf and thyme into the cavity.
5. Brush the chicken with the melted butter and then place it in the chicken stand.
6. Close the lid and cook for 10 minutes.
7. After 10 minutes, blend with the Brandy and the wine, close the lid and cook for another 60 minutes.
8. Turn the chicken from time to time and sprinkle it with the cooking juices.
9. Once cooked, remove the chicken from the grill and support and place it on a cutting board.
10. Let it rest for 5 minutes, then cut it into pieces and put it on serving plates.
11. Sprinkle with the cooking juices and serve.

TIPS: I recommend that you combine this recipe with Griddle asparagus

Chicken griddle kebab

**20 MINUTES
+ 15' REST**

24 MINUTES

4

INGREDIENTS

» 28.2 oz of chicken breast
» 1 onion
» 1 tsp of cinnamon powder
» ½ tsp of turmeric powder
» Tartar sauce to taste
» Salt and pepper to taste
» Olive oil to taste
» 4 Nani bread

DIRECTIONS

1. Peel and wash the onion and then chop it.
2. Put the cinnamon, turmeric, onion, salt, pepper and 4 tablespoons of olive oil in a bowl.
3. Mix well, then wash the chicken, cut it into cubes and put it in the bowl.
4. Mix well and put in the fridge to marinate for 3 hours.
5. After 3 hours, take the meat out of the fridge and put the skewers together.
6. Fill all the skewers until you have finished all the chicken cubes.
7. Preheat the grill to 392 ° F for 10 minutes.
8. Oil the grill and place the skewers on top.
9. Close the lid and cook for 15 minutes, turning and brushing with the marinade often.
10. Once cooked, put the kebabs on serving plates, add the Nani bread and tartar sauce and serve.

Griddle chicken curry with peppers

PREPARATION: 20 MINUTES
COOKING: 50 MINUTES
PORTIONS: 4

INGREDIENTS

» 28.2 oz of chicken breast
» 2 cups of vegetable broth
» 1 yellow pepper
» 4.4 oz of Greek yogurt
» 1 red pepper
» 3 tsp of curry powder
» 1 onion
» 1 tsp of cinnamon powder
» Salt and pepper to taste
» Olive oil to taste

DIRECTIONS

1. Preheat the grill to 392 ° F for 10 minutes.
2. Wash the chicken breast and then cut it into cubes.
3. Peel, wash and then cut the onion into cubes.
4. Wash the peppers, remove the cap, divide them in half, remove the seeds and white filaments and cut them into cubes.
5. When the grill is hot enough, put a cast iron saucepan on top and let it heat up.
6. When the saucepan is hot, add 3 tablespoons of olive oil.
7. As soon as the oil begins to bubble, add the chicken, and brown it for a couple of minutes.
8. Season with salt and pepper and add the onion, curry, and cinnamon.
9. Put the broth, cover with the lid and switch to indirect cooking.
10. Cook for 20 minutes, stirring occasionally.
11. After 20 minutes, add the peppers and continue to cook for another 20 minutes.
12. Now add the yogurt and cook for another 5 minutes.
13. After cooking, remove the saucepan from the grill and let it rest for 5 minutes.
14. Now put the chicken on the plates, sprinkle with the cooking juices and serve.

Griddle chicken fajitas with peppers

PREPARATION: 20 MINUTES
COOKING: 35 MINUTES
PORTIONS: 4

INGREDIENTS

» 4 tortillas
» 28.2 oz of chicken breast
» 2 tbsp of caraway seeds
» 1 yellow pepper
» 1 red pepper
» 1 green pepper
» 1 white onion
» Salt and pepper to taste
» Mayonnaise to taste
» Olive oil to taste

DIRECTIONS

1. Preheat the grill to 392 ° F for 10 minutes.
2. Wash and dry the chicken, remove the excess fat, and divide it in half.
3. Brush the meat with olive oil and season with salt and pepper.
4. Remove the cap and the seeds from the peppers and then cut them into layers.
5. Peel, wash and thinly slice the onion.
6. When the grill is hot enough, place the chicken and grill it for 10 minutes on each side.
7. Once cooked, wrap it in aluminum foil and let it rest.
8. Put a cast iron pan with 3 tablespoons of olive oil and let it heat up.
9. Put the onion and let it brown for 5 minutes.
10. Put the peppers, and sauté them for 5 minutes.
11. Season with salt and pepper and remove the pan from the grill.
12. Put the tortillas and let them heat 1 minute on each side, then remove them and put them on the plates.
13. Now cut the chicken into thin slices.
14. Put the chicken, onion, and peppers inside the tortillas.
15. Sprinkle with mayonnaise, close the tortillas and serve.

Griddle duck breast with cognac

10 MINUTES
+ 1 H REST

5 MINUTES

4

INGREDIENTS

- » 2 duck breasts of 10.5 oz each
- » 1 tbsp of melted butter
- » 1 glass of Cognac
- » 2 sprigs of thyme
- » Salt and pepper to taste

DIRECTIONS

1. Wash and dry the thyme and put it in a bowl.
2. Score the duck skin and place it in the bowl with the thyme.
3. Add the cognac, salt, pepper, and butter.
4. Refrigerate and marinate for 1 hour
5. Pass the hour, take the duck out of the fridge, and preheat the grill to 320 ° F for 10 minutes.
6. When the grill is ready, oil it and put the marinated duck breasts with the skin facing up.
7. Cook for 20 minutes, turning the duck halfway through cooking and brushing it often with the marinade.
8. When the internal temperature of the duck has reached 136 ° F, you can remove it from the grill and put it on a cutting board.
9. Cut the duck into slices, put them on serving plates and serve.

TIPS: You can combine this recipe with Griddle soy noodles with vegetables

Griddle honey chicken skewers

20 MINUTES + 3 H REST

12 MINUTES

4

INGREDIENTS

» 21.1 oz of chicken breast
» 2 cloves of garlic
» 2 glasses of whole milk
» 2 sage leaves
» 2 sprigs of thyme
» 1 glass of white wine
» 1 tablespoon of honey
» 1 lemon
» 2 sprigs of rosemary
» Salt and pepper to taste
» Olive oil to taste

DIRECTIONS

1. Wash the chicken breast and then cut it into cubes.
2. Peel and chop the garlic cloves.
3. Wash and dry sage, thyme, and rosemary.
4. Put the milk in a bowl and add the chicken, salt, pepper, aromatic herbs and garlic.
5. Mix well, refrigerate, and marinate for 3 hours.
6. After 3 hours, take the chicken out of the fridge.
7. Preheat the grill to 392 ° F for 10 minutes.
8. Drain the chicken cubes, dry them, and stick them on the skewers.
9. Put the wine, the filtered lemon juice and the honey in a bowl and mix well until the honey has completely dissolved.
10. Brush the skewers with the wine and honey and place them on the grill.
11. Cook for 3 minutes on each side, constantly brushing with the honey sauce.
12. Once cooked, remove the skewers from the grill, place them on serving plates and serve.

TIPS: You can combine this recipe with Griddle Zucchini Cheeseburgers

Griddle turkey breast with Greek yogurt and saffron

INGREDIENTS

» 21.1 oz of turkey breast
» 5.9 oz of Greek yogurt
» 2 tsp of saffron
» 1 lemon
» 1 shallot
» 1 sprig of wild fennel
» 1 clove of garlic
» Olive oil to taste
» Salt and pepper to taste

DIRECTIONS

1. Wash and dry the turkey and then divide it in half.
2. Peel the shallot and garlic, wash them, and cut them into thin slices.
3. Put the turkey in a bowl, add the shallot, garlic, fennel, salt, pepper, olive oil and the filtered lemon juice.
4. Marinate at room temperature for 30 minutes.
5. Preheat the grill to 356 ° F for 10 minutes.
6. When the grill is ready, add the turkey breast and cook for 10 minutes per side.
7. Meanwhile, make the yogurt and saffron sauce.
8. Put the yogurt, salt, pepper, saffron and 2 tablespoons of olive oil in a bowl.
9. Stir until you get a thick and homogeneous sauce.
10. When the turkey is cooked, remove it from the grill and place it on a cutting board.
11. Let it rest for a few minutes, then cut it into slices and put it on serving plates.
12. Sprinkle with the saffron sauce and serve.

TIPS: You can combine this recipe with Sauteed griddle peppers with soy sauce

20 MINUTES
+ 30 REST

15 MINUTES

4

Griddle turkey stew with smoked bacon and peas

15 MINUTES

45 MINUTES

4

INGREDIENTS

» 24.6 oz of turkey breast
» 14.1 oz of frozen peas
» 3.5 oz of bacon
» 1 oz of butter
» 1 sprig of thyme
» 1 clove garlic
» 2 cups of vegetable broth
» Flour to taste
» Salt and pepper to taste

DIRECTIONS

1. Preheat the grill to 356 ° F for 10 minutes.
2. Meanwhile, wash and dry the turkey and cut it into cubes.
3. Put the flour on a plate and flour the turkey cubes.
4. Peel and chop the garlic.
5. Wash and dry the rosemary.
6. When the grill is ready, put a cast iron saucepan on top and let it heat up.
7. As soon as the saucepan is hot enough, add the butter and let it melt.
8. Add the garlic and diced bacon and cook for a couple of minutes.
9. Now add the turkey and brown it for 5 minutes.
10. Add the broth, put the lid on and switch to indirect cooking.
11. Cook for 30 minutes, stirring occasionally.
12. After 30 minutes, add the peas and thyme and season with salt and pepper.
13. Cook for another 10 minutes, then remove the saucepan from the grill and let it rest for 5 minutes.
14. Remove the thyme, put the stew on serving plates and serve.

Hibachi griddle chicken

15 MINUTES

10 MINUTES

4

INGREDIENTS

- » 28 oz of chicken breast
- » 4 tbsp of olive oil
- » 8 shitake mushrooms
- » 4 tablespoons of butter
- » 1 lemon
- » 2 tbsp of mixed sesame seeds
- » Salt and pepper to taste

DIRECTIONS

1. Place the griddle on the grill and let it preheat at 400 ° F for 10 minutes.
2. Meanwhile, wash the mushrooms, dry them and cut them into slices.
3. Wash and dry the chicken and then cut it into cubes.
4. Put the mushrooms and chicken in a bowl and season with salt and pepper.
5. When the plate is hot, brush it with olive oil.
6. Then add the chicken and mushrooms and cook for 8 minutes, stirring often.
7. Now add the butter and sesame seeds and continue cooking until the butter has completely melted.
8. Put the chicken and mushrooms on the serving plates.
9. Sprinkle with sesame seeds and serve.

Mexican style marinated griddle chicken wings

15 MINUTES
+ 3 H REST

30 MINUTES

4

INGREDIENTS

- » 12 chicken wings
- » 4.5 oz of ketchup
- » 3 tbsp of brown sugar
- » 1 tsp of coriander seeds
- » 1 tsp of cumin
- » ½ glass of apple cider vinegar
- » 1 onion
- » 1 tsp of tabasco
- » Olive oil to taste
- » Salt and pepper to taste

DIRECTIONS

1. Wash and dry the chicken wings and remove the skin.
2. Put them in a bowl and add the ketchup, salt, pepper, brown sugar, Tabasco, vinegar, cumin and coriander.
3. Peel and wash the onion, chop it and put it in the bowl with the wings.
4. Add 4 tablespoons of olive oil and mix well.
5. Put the bowl in the fridge and marinate for 3 hours.
6. After 3 hours, take the chicken wings out of the fridge and preheat the grill to 428 ° F for 10 minutes.
7. When the grill is ready, put the wings on and cook for 30 minutes.
8. Turn the chicken wings often and brush them with the marinade.
9. Once cooked, remove the chicken wings from the grill and let them rest for 5 minutes.
10. Now put the chicken wings on the serving plates and serve.

Beef and chicken griddle tortillas

PREPARATION: 25' + 1 H REST
COOKING: 25 MINUTES
PORTIONS: 4

INGREDIENTS

» 4 tortillas
» 7 oz of beef sirloin
» 7 oz of chicken breast
» 7 oz of yellow peppers
» 7 oz of red peppers
» 1 lime
» 1 white onion
» 1 tsp of Worcestershire sauce
» 4 slices of cheddar
» Guacamole to taste
» 2 tsp of coriander
» 1 tsp of cumin
» Salt and pepper to taste

DIRECTIONS

1. Cut the beef and chicken into thin slices and place them in a bowl.
2. Wash and dry the lime. Grate the zest and strain the juice into the bowl with the meat.
3. Also add the chopped coriander, cumin, salt, and pepper.
4. Mix with your hands to flavor everything well, then cover the bowl with cling film and leave to marinate in the refrigerator for an hour.
5. Meanwhile, peel and wash the onion and then cut it into thin slices.
6. Remove the cap and the seeds from the peppers, wash them and then cut them into slices.
7. After the hour, remove the meat from the fridge and let it rest at room temperature.
8. Preheat the grill to 392 ° F for 10 minutes.
9. Put a cast iron saucepan on the grill and let it heat up.
10. Put 2 tablespoons of olive oil, let it heat up and then add the onion and peppers.
11. Cook for 10 minutes, stirring often.
12. At this point add the meat and brown it well.
13. Then deglaze with the Worcestershire sauce and cook for about 5-6 minutes.
14. After cooking, remove the saucepan and put the tortillas.
15. Cook for 1 minute, then turn them over and add the cheddar.
16. Cook until the cheese has melted, then remove them from the grill and place them on plates.
17. Divide the filling into the tortillas, add the guacamole, close the flaps of the tortilla over the filling and serve.

Beef and vegetable griddle burrito

PREPARATION: 15 MINUTES
COOKING: 30 MINUTES
PORTIONS: 4

INGREDIENTS

» 4 tortillas
» 14 oz of minced beef
» 1 white onion
» 4 sweet green chilies
» 5.2 oz of corn kernels
» 4 slices of Cheddar
» 1 red pepper
» 1 glass of vegetable broth
» 14 oz of cooked black beans
» Sale to taste
» Chilli to taste
» Olive oil to taste

DIRECTIONS

1. Preheat the grill to 356 ° F for 10 minutes.
2. Meanwhile, peel and wash the onion and then chop it.
3. Remove the cap and the seeds from the peppers and red pepper and then cut them into cubes.
4. When the grill is hot, put a cast iron saucepan and let it heat up.
5. As soon as the saucepan has heated up, add 3 tablespoons of olive oil.
6. When the oil is hot, add the onion and cook it for 5 minutes.
7. Add the meat, mix well and brown for 5 minutes.
8. Add the chilies and pepper and cook for another 5 minutes.
9. Finally add the beans and corn and season with salt and add the chili.
10. Add the vegetable broth and put the lid on the saucepan.
11. Switch to indirect cooking and cook for 15 minutes.
12. Once cooked, remove the saucepan from the grill and place the tortillas.
13. Toast for a minute on each side, then remove them from the grill and place them on plates.
14. Place the cheddar and then the meat on the tortillas.
15. Close the stuffed tortillas forming a roll and serve.

Beef griddle teppanyaki with mixed vegetables

20 MINUTES

10 MINUTES

4

INGREDIENTS

- » 14 oz of beef tenderloin
- » 1 minced clove of garlic
- » 2 tbsp of mirin
- » 7 oz of bamboo shoots
- » 7 oz of pumpkin pulp
- » 3.5 oz of shitake mushrooms
- » 6 spring onions
- » 1 red pepper
- » Sesame seed oil
- » Salt and pepper to taste
- » Soy sauce to taste

DIRECTIONS

1. Put the mirin, 3 tablespoons of soy sauce and the garlic in a bowl. Stir until you get a homogeneous emulsion.
2. Wash and dry the fillet. Cut the meat into thin slices and make a large crosscut on each slice; place them on a large serving dish with the soy sauce.
3. Put the meat in the fridge and marinate for 1 hour.
4. Meanwhile, remove the ends of the spring onions and then wash them and cut them into thin slices.
5. Wash the pumpkin pulp and cut it into thin slices.
6. Wash the mushrooms, dry them, and cut them into small pieces.
7. Remove the cap and the seeds from the pepper, wash it and cut it into cubes.
8. Place the griddle on the grill and preheat it to 392 ° F for 10 minutes.
9. When the griddle is hot, brush it with plenty of oil and add the meat and vegetables.
10. Cook the vegetables and meat for 10 minutes, turning it halfway through cooking.
11. After cooking, put the meat and vegetables on serving plates.
12. Sprinkle with soy sauce and serve.

Griddle beef entrecote with yogurt and olive sauce

15 MINUTES

15 MINUTES

4

INGREDIENTS

» 21.1 oz of sirloin of beef
» 5.2 oz of Greek yogurt
» 2 tbsp of chopped chives
» 3 tbsp of chopped mixed herbs
» 12 black olives
» 2 tbsp of Cognac
» Salt and pepper to taste
» Olive oil to taste

DIRECTIONS

1. Preheat the grill to 446 ° F for 10 minutes.
2. Brush the meat with olive oil and season with salt, pepper and chopped aromatic herbs.
3. Chop the olives and set aside.
4. When the grill is hot, put the meat and cook, direct cooking, for about ten minutes, turning the meat often.
5. When the core temperature of the meat is 131 ° F you can take it off the grill.
6. Put it on a cutting board, wrap it in aluminum foil and let it rest for 10 minutes.
7. Put the Cognac, yogurt, olives, and chives in a cast iron pan.
8. Cook for 5 minutes, stirring constantly and then remove the saucepan from the grill.
9. Now cut the meat into thin slices, put the meat on plates, sprinkle with the olive sauce and serve.

TIPS: You can combine this recipe with Sauteed griddle peppers with soy sauce

Griddle beef roast with bacon

INGREDIENTS

- » 28.2 oz of beef tenderloin
- » 3 lemons
- » 3.5 oz of bacon
- » ½ glass of white wine
- » 4 bay leaves
- » Salt and pepper to taste
- » Olive oil to taste

DIRECTIONS

1. Preheat the grill to 356 ° F for 10 minutes.
2. Wash and dry the beef fillet, brush it with olive oil and season with salt and pepper.
3. Place the bacon slices on a sheet of parchment paper, side by side.
4. Place the beef fillet on top and wrap it with the slices of speck.
5. Wash and dry the bay leaves.
6. Tie the roast with kitchen twine and place the bay leaves between the twine and the meat.
7. Put the meat on the roasting rack.
8. Put the support on the grill, switch to indirect cooking and cook for 50 minutes.
9. Put the wine, the filtered lemon juice, oil, salt, and pepper in a bowl. Stir until you get a homogeneous emulsion.
10. Brush the meat every 10 minutes with the wine and lemon emulsion.
11. When the core temperature of the meat has reached 131 ° F, you can remove it from the grill.
12. Let the roast rest for 5 minutes on a cutting board and then remove the string and bay leaf.
13. Cut the roast into slices, put it on serving plates and serve.

TIPS: I recommend that you combine this recipe with Griddle flavored potatoes

15 MINUTES

50 MINUTES

4

Grilled beef with Greek sauce

PREPARATION: 25 MINUTES
COOKING: 1 HOUR
PORTIONS: 4

INGREDIENTS

- » 28.2 oz of beef tenderloin
- » 5.2 oz of Greek yogurt
- » 3.5 oz of feta
- » 6 mint leaves
- » 1 garlic clove, minced
- » 1 head of lettuce
- » 20 cherry tomatoes
- » 2 red onions
- » Olive oil to taste
- » Salt and pepper to taste

DIRECTIONS

1. Preheat the grill to 356 ° F for 10 minutes.
2. Wash and dry the beef tenderloin and remove the excess fat.
3. Brush the meat with olive oil and season with salt and pepper.
4. When the grill is hot, put the fillet, switch to indirect cooking, close the lid and cook for 1 hour.
5. Meanwhile, make the Greek sauce.
6. Crumble the feta cheese, put it in a bowl and add the Greek yogurt, minced garlic, chopped mint, a drizzle of olive oil, salt, and pepper.
7. Now wash the tomatoes and then cut them into wedges.
8. Wash and dry the lettuce leaves and then cut them into small pieces.
9. Peel and wash the onions and then cut them into thin slices.
10. Put the onions, cherry tomatoes and lettuce divided into 4 serving plates and season with oil, salt and pepper.
11. When the beef is cooked, remove it from the grill and place it on a cutting board.
12. Let it rest for 5 minutes, and then cut the meat into cubes.
13. Place the meat cubes on top of the salad, sprinkle with the Greek sauce and serve.

Griddle entrecote with mustard and sage cream

15 MINUTES

12 MINUTES

4

INGREDIENTS

- » 2 ribs of beef of 14 oz each
- » 1 glass of whole milk
- » 12 sage leaves
- » 2 tbsp rustic mustard with seeds
- » Olive oil to taste
- » Salt and pepper to taste

DIRECTIONS

1. Preheat the grill to 500 °F for 10 minutes.
2. Wash and dry the sage leaves and then chop them.
3. Wash and dry the meat, brush it with olive oil and season with salt and pepper and the chopped sage.
4. When the grill is ready, place the ribs and cook 6 minutes per side, or until the core temperature of the meat reaches 131 °F.
5. After cooking, remove the meat from the grill, put it on a cutting board and let it rest for 5 minutes.
6. Now cut the ribs and slices and place them on serving plates.
7. Put the mustard in a bowl and add oil, salt, and pepper.
8. Mix well and then pour the sauce over the meat and serve.
9. TIPS: I recommend that you combine this recipe with Griddle green beans and eggs

Hibachi grilled beef and shrimps

20 MINUTES
+ 30' REST

- MINUTES

4

INGREDIENTS

» 1 tbsp of sesame seed oil
» 3 tbsp of olive oil
» ½ glass of mirin
» 2 tbsp of soy sauce
» 21 oz of beef sirloin
» ½ lemon
» 21 oz of shrimp
» 1 tbsp of chopped parsley
» Salt and pepper to taste

DIRECTIONS

1. Put the olive oil, sesame seed oil, mirin and soy sauce in a bowl and mix well.
2. Shell the prawns, wash them and then put them in a bowl.
3. Cut the beef sirloin and place it in the bowl with the prawns.
4. Season with salt and pepper and then add the soy emulsion and the filtered lemon juice.
5. Mix well and leave to marinate for 30 minutes.
6. After 30 minutes, place the griddle on the grill and preheat it at 360 ° F for 10 minutes.
7. When the plate is hot, put the meat and prawns to cook.
8. Cook for 8 minutes, stirring often.
9. Put the meat and shrimp on the plates, sprinkle with the chopped parsley and serve.

Hibachi griddle beef noodles

20 MINUTES + 30' REST

25 MINUTES

4

INGREDIENTS

- » 21 oz of lo Mein noodles
- » 14 oz of beef tenderloin
- » 1 glass of soy sauce
- » 4 tsp of grated ginger
- » 4 tsp of garlic powder
- » 8 tsp of corn starch
- » 4 tbsp of brown sugar
- » Chopped chives to taste
- » 8 cloves
- » 4 tsp of sesame oil
- » 4 tbsp of butter
- » Salt and pepper to taste

DIRECTIONS

1. Wash and dry the meat, cut it into cubes and put it in a bowl.
2. In another bowl, combine the soy sauce, sugar, garlic and ginger powder, cloves, cornstarch, oil, salt, and pepper and mix well.
3. Pour the emulsion over the meat, mix, and then leave to marinate for 30 minutes.
4. Place the griddle on the grill and preheat it to 392 ° F for 10 minutes.
5. When the griddle is hot, put a cast iron saucepan with water and salt on top and bring to a boil. Then pour in the noodles and cook for 10 minutes.
6. After 10 minutes, remove the saucepan from the grill, drain the noodles and set aside.
7. Now put the meat on the grill, drain and cook for 5 minutes, stirring often.
8. Put the noodles, add the butter, and cook until it is completely melted.
9. Now pour in the filtered marinating liquid and cook until it is completely absorbed by the noodles.
10. Once cooked, put the noodles and the meat on the serving plates.
11. Sprinkle with the chives and serve.

Mexican-style griddle beef tacos

10 MINUTES

20 MINUTES

4

INGREDIENTS

- » 17.6 oz of minced beef
- » 12 tacos
- » 8 lettuce leaves
- » 1 onion
- » 6.3 oz of grated cheddar
- » ½ glass of white wine
- » 3.5 oz of Mexican salsa
- » Salt and pepper to taste
- » Olive oil to taste

DIRECTIONS

1. Preheat the grill to 392 ° F.
2. Meanwhile, peel and wash the onion and then chop it.
3. Wash and dry the lettuce leaves and then cut them into thin slices.
4. When the grill is hot enough, put a cast iron saucepan on top and let it heat up.
5. Then add two tablespoons of olive oil and, when it is hot, add the onion.
6. Sauté for 5 minutes and then add the meat.
7. Mix well, cook for 5 minutes, and then blend with the white wine.
8. When the wine has evaporated, add the Mexican sauce, and cook for another 10 minutes.
9. After cooking, remove the saucepan from the grill and set aside.
10. Place the tacos on the grill and heat them for 2 minutes.
11. Put 3 tacos on each plate. Fill them with lettuce and meat.
12. Sprinkle with grated cheddar and serve.

Rib eye steak griddle with honey glaze

INGREDIENTS

» 28.2 oz of rib eye steak
» 1 clove of garlic
» 2 sprigs of thyme
» 1 tsp of sweet paprika
» 1 tbsp of honey
» ½ glass of white wine
» Olive oil to taste
» Salt and pepper to taste

DIRECTIONS

1. Preheat the grill to 482 ° F.
2. Peel, wash and chop the garlic.
3. Wash the thyme, remove the leaves and then chop them.
4. Brush the steak with olive oil and then sprinkle the entire surface with salt, pepper, garlic and chopped thyme.
5. When the grill is hot, oil it and put the steak on top.
6. Cook 3 minutes on each side or until the core temperature of the meat reaches 131 ° F.
7. Meanwhile, put the honey, wine, salt, pepper and paprika in a cast iron saucepan.
8. Put the saucepan on the grill and cook for 5 minutes.
9. After cooking, put the meat on a cutting board and let it rest for 5 minutes.
10. Cut the steak into slices and place them on plates.
11. Brush the meat with the honey glaze and serve.
12. TIPS: I recommend that you combine this recipe with soft griddle potato pie

15 MINUTES

10 MINUTES

4

Jerk pork griddle with avocado sauce

20 MINUTES + 2 H REST

20 MINUTES

4

INGREDIENTS

- » 4 pork chops
- » 1 clove of garlic
- » 1 bay leaf
- » 1 avocado
- » ½ cucumber
- » 1 lime
- » 1 chopped chili
- » 2 sprigs of thyme
- » 1 tomato
- » 2 spring onions
- » Salt and pepper to taste
- » Olive oil to taste

DIRECTIONS

1. Wash and dry the spring onions and then chop them.
2. Peel the garlic and then chop it.
3. Wash and dry the thyme and bay leaves and then chop them.
4. Put the pork chops in a bowl. Add salt, pepper, chili, olive oil, the chopped garlic, spring onions, thyme and bay leaves and put the bowl in the fridge.
5. Marinate for 2 hours.
6. After 2 hours, take the meat out of the fridge and preheat the grill to 356 ° F for 10 minutes.
7. When the grill is ready, place the chops and cook for 10 minutes per side.
8. Meanwhile, wash the tomato and then cut it into cubes.
9. Also peel the avocado and cucumber and cut them into small pieces.
10. Put the tomato, avocado, and cucumber in a bowl.
11. Add the filtered lime juice, salt, pepper, and olive oil and mix everything well.
12. When the chops are ready, remove them from the grill and let them rest for 5 minutes.
13. Now put the chops on the plates, sprinkle with the sauce and serve.

Griddle lamb chops with raspberry and balsamic sauce

15 MINUTES + 1 H REST

15 MINUTES

4

INGREDIENTS

- » 8.8 oz of raspberries
- » 4 lamb chops of 3.5 oz each
- » 4 tbsp of butter
- » 1 tbsp of chopped chives
- » 1 glass of white wine
- » 1 clove of minced garlic
- » Salt and pepper to taste
- » Balsamic vinegar to taste

DIRECTIONS

1. Wash and dry the raspberries, put them in the blender and blend them.
2. Sieve the raspberries and strain the juice into a bowl.
3. Wash and dry the ribs, remove the excess fat and then put them in the bowl with the raspberry juice.
4. Add salt, pepper, wine and the minced garlic clove.
5. Stir and put in the fridge to marinate for 1 hour.
6. After the hour, take the meat out of the fridge and preheat the grill to 356 ° F for 10 minutes.
7. When the grill is hot enough, put the cutlets drained from the marinade.
8. Cook for 5 minutes on each side, then remove them from the grill and let them rest.
9. Put the marinating liquid in a cast iron saucepan, put it on the grill and bring to a boil.
10. Remove the saucepan from the grill, add the butter and stir until completely melted.
11. Put the ribs on the plates, sprinkle them with the raspberry sauce and serve.

Rum griddle pork chops

PREPARATION: 15 MINUTES
REST TIME: 3 HOURS
COOKING: 30 MINUTES
PORTIONS: 4

INGREDIENTS

» 4 pork chops of 7 oz each
» 2 oranges
» 1.4 oz of butter
» 1 lemon
» ½ glass of rum
» 1 tbsp of chopped parsley
» Salt and pepper to taste
» Olive oil to taste

DIRECTIONS

1. Squeeze and strain the oranges juice and lemon into a bowl.
2. Add oil, salt and pepper and mix well.
3. Wash the chops, remove the excess fat and place them in the bowl with the marinade.
4. Sprinkle with rum, refrigerate and marinate for 3 hours.
5. After 3 hours, take the meat out of the fridge and put the grill to heat at 374 ° F for 10 minutes.
6. When the grill is hot, place the chops and cook 5 minutes on each side, or until the core temperature of the meat reaches 149 ° F.
7. After cooking, remove the meat from the grill and let it rest.
8. In the meantime, take the marinade, put it in a cast iron pan.
9. Put the saucepan on the grill and bring to a boil.
10. Remove the saucepan from the grill, add the butter and chopped parsley, and stir until the butter has completely melted.
11. Put the chops on the plates, sprinkle them with the rum sauce and serve.

TIPS: you can combine this recipe with Griddle pineapple upside down pie

Tikka griddle kebab

PREPARATION: 20 MINUTES
REST TIME: 12 HOURS
COOKING: 20 MINUTES
PORTIONS: 4

INGREDIENTS

- » 24.6 oz of lamb shoulder
- » ½ cup of Greek yogurt
- » 2 green peppers
- » 2 lemons
- » 5 onions
- » 3 cloves of garlic
- » 1 tsp of turmeric
- » 1 tbsp of white vinegar
- » 1 tbsp of sugar
- » Salt and pepper to taste

DIRECTIONS

1. Peel and wash the garlic and onion. Put them in the mixer and add the juice of a lemon, the turmeric, the vinegar, and the yogurt.
2. Blend everything until you get a smooth sauce.
3. Wash the lamb, remove the fat, and cut it into cubes.
4. Put the meat in a bowl, season with salt, pepper and sugar and mix.
5. Cover with the yogurt sauce and refrigerate to marinate overnight.
6. After the marinating time, take the meat out of the fridge.
7. Preheat the grill to 392 ° F for 10 minutes.
8. Remove the seeds and cap from the peppers, wash them and then cut them into cubes.
9. Now start forming the skewers alternating the lamb morsels with pieces of pepper.
10. Oil the grill and place the skewers on top.
11. Close the lid and cook for 20 minutes, turning the meat often.
12. Once cooked, remove the skewers from the grill and place them on serving plates.
13. Dress with a drizzle of raw oil and serve.

Kuzu griddle kebab

PREPARATION: 30 MINUTES
REST TIME: 6 HOURS
COOKING: 15 MINUTES
PORTIONS: 4

INGREDIENTS

» 24.6 oz of lamb shoulder
» 2 cloves of garlic
» 1 cup of Greek yogurt
» 8 cherry tomatoes
» 6 green peppers
» 4 red onions
» 4 pitas
» Salt and pepper to taste
» Olive oil to taste

DIRECTIONS

1. Meanwhile, wash the meat, remove the excess fat and then cut it into cubes.
2. Peel the garlic, chop it and put it in a bowl.
3. Add the yogurt, salt and pepper and mix well.
4. Put the meat in the bowl with the yogurt and mix.
5. Cover the bowl and leave to marinate in the fridge for 6 hours.
6. After 6 hours, remove the meat from the fridge.
7. Preheat the grill to 392 ° F for 10 minutes.
8. Meanwhile, wash the cherry tomatoes and cut them in half.
9. Peel and wash the onions and cut them into 4 parts.
10. Remove the cap and the seeds from the peppers and then cut them into cubes.
11. Take the steel skewers and arrange them in the following order: red pepper, onion, meat, tomato and green pepper.
12. Repeat the operation for the other skewers as well until all the ingredients have been used up.
13. Oil the grill and place the skewers on top.
14. Close the lid and cook for 15 minutes, turning the skewers often.
15. After cooking, remove the skewers from the grill.
16. Put the skewers on the plates, add the pitas, season with a drizzle of oil and serve.

TIPS: I recommend you combine this Griddle pumpkin recipe

Griddle asparagus

15 MINUTES

4 MINUTES

4

INGREDIENTS

» 8.8 oz of green asparagus
» 8.8 oz of white asparagus
» 1 tbsp of toasted white sesame seeds
» 1 tbsp of toasted black sesame seeds
» Mayonnaise to taste
» Salt and pepper to taste
» Olive oil to taste

DIRECTIONS

1. Preheat the grill to 356 ° F for 10 minutes.
2. Remove the woody part of the asparagus and then wash them.
3. Put the asparagus in a bowl, season with oil, salt and pepper and mix well.
4. Arrange the asparagus on the grill and cook for 2 minutes per side.
5. When the asparagus are well cooked, remove them from the grill and place them on serving plates.
6. Season with a few sprigs of mayonnaise, sprinkle with sesame seeds and serve.

Griddle breaded eggplant

10 MINUTES

15 MINUTES

4

INGREDIENTS

- » 2 eggplants
- » 3 tbsp of milk
- » 2 eggs
- » 8.8 oz of breadcrumbs
- » 4.2 oz of flour
- » Olive oil to taste
- » Salt and pepper to taste

DIRECTIONS

1. Beat the egg and milk together in a shallow dish.
2. Combine the breadcrumbs, salt, and pepper on a separate plate.
3. Wash and cut the eggplants into thick slices.
4. Cover the eggplant slices with flour, then dip them in the egg and bread them with breadcrumbs. Dip in the egg and breadcrumbs again.
5. Brush each side of the eggplant slices with olive oil.
6. Place the breaded eggplants directly on the grill.
7. Cook the eggplants for 10 minutes.
8. Turn the eggplants over halfway through cooking and as soon as they are ready, take them off the grill.
9. Let them rest for a few minutes and serve them on serving plates with sauce of your choice.

Griddle feta with oriental sauce

INGREDIENTS

» 14.1 oz of feta cheese
» ½ glass of soy sauce
» 1 tbsp of apple cider vinegar
» 1 tbsp of balsamic vinegar
» 2 tbsp of olive oil
» 2 tbsp of honey
» 1 tbsp of chopped chives
» 2 tsp of paprika in spicy

DIRECTIONS

1. First, take the feta and cut it into cubes or strips if you prefer.
2. Meanwhile, prepare the marinade sauce.
3. Then mix the honey, apple cider vinegar, olive oil, soy sauce, and paprika.
4. Mix the ingredients well until they are completely blended.
5. Brush the cubes or strips of feta with the freshly prepared sauce and let them marinate for 15 minutes.
6. Meanwhile, preheat the grill to 374 ° F.
7. When the temperature is reached, place the feta cubes drained from the marinade on the grill.
8. Close the lid and leave to grill for 5 minutes per side.
9. After cooking, remove the feta from the grill and place on serving plates.
10. Serve the feta cubes immediately with the cooking sauce and the chopped chives sprinkled on top.

15 MINUTES

10 MINUTES

4

Griddle flavored potatoes

15 MINUTES

30 MINUTES

4

INGREDIENTS

- » 28.2 oz of potatoes
- » 1 tbsp of chopped thyme
- » 1.4 oz of butter
- » 2 bay leaves
- » 1 tsp of pink peppercorns
- » 1 tsp of green peppercorns
- » 1 clove garlic
- » Salt and pepper to taste
- » Olive oil to taste

DIRECTIONS

1. Preheat the grill to 392 ° F.
2. Meanwhile, wash and dry the potatoes and then cut them into cubes.
3. Wash and dry the bay leaves and then chop them.
4. Peel the garlic clove and then chop it.
5. Brush 4 aluminum foil leaves with olive oil.
6. Divide the potato cubes within each sheet.
7. Sprinkle with thyme, bay leaf, garlic, pink and green pepper, salt, and pepper.
8. Drizzle with olive oil, add a few knobs of butter and close the packets.
9. Place the parcels on the grill, close the lid and cook for 30 minutes.
10. After cooking, remove the packets from the grill and leave to rest for 5 minutes.
11. Put the parcels in serving dishes, open them carefully to avoid burning yourself and serve.

Griddle green beans and eggs

10 MINUTES

20 MINUTES

4

INGREDIENTS

- » 17.6 oz of boiled green beans
- » 1 onion
- » 2 eggs
- » 2 tbsp of grated parmesan
- » Olive oil to taste
- » Salt and pepper to taste

DIRECTIONS

1. Preheat the grill to 356 ° F for 10 minutes.
2. Cut the green beans in half.
3. Peel and wash the onion then cut it into thin slices.
4. Place a cast iron skillet on the grill and add 3 tablespoons of olive oil.
5. When the oil is hot, add the onion and cook for 5 minutes.
6. Now put the green beans, season with salt and pepper, close the pan with the lid and cook for 5 minutes.
7. While the green beans are cooking, break the eggs into a bowl, add the parmesan, salt, and pepper.
8. Beat everything with a fork until the mixture is smooth.
9. After 5 minutes, pour the beaten eggs directly into the pan with the green beans.
10. Stir constantly and cook for another 4 minutes.
11. Remove the pan from the grill, place the green beans and eggs on the plates and serve.

Griddle potato gratin

10 MINUTES

10 MINUTES

4

INGREDIENTS

» 35 oz of boiled potatoes
» 2 glasses of bechamel
» 17.6 oz of mozzarella
» 7 oz of grated Parmesan cheese
» 2 tbsp of chopped parsley
» 4 tbsp of breadcrumbs
» Salt and pepper to taste
» Olive oil to taste

DIRECTIONS

1. Preheat the grill to 392 ° F.
2. Peel the potatoes and then cut them into slices.
3. Take a cast iron saucepan and brush it with olive oil.
4. Put on the bottom of the casserole with a little of the breadcrumbs bechamel.
5. Begin to form the first layer with the potatoes, season with salt and pepper, cover with slices of mozzarella, a ladle of bechamel and a little grated Parmesan.
6. Repeat the steps alternating the ingredients until you finish with a layer of potatoes.
7. Cover everything with béchamel and breadcrumbs and then sprinkle the surface with chopped parsley.
8. Put the saucepan on the grill, cover with the lid and cook for 15 minutes.
9. After cooking, remove the saucepan from the grill and let it rest for 5 minutes.
10. Put the potatoes into serving plates and serve.

Griddle potatoes with curry

INGREDIENTS

- » 17.6 oz of potatoes
- » 2 tsp of curry powder
- » 1 tsp of chopped chili
- » 1 cup of vegetable broth
- » 1 clove garlic
- » Chopped chives to taste
- » Olive oil to taste
- » Salt and pepper to taste

DIRECTIONS

1. Preheat the grill to 374 ° F.
2. Peel and wash the potatoes and then cut them into cubes.
3. Peel the garlic and then chop it.
4. Put a cast iron saucepan with 2 tablespoons of olive oil on the grill and heat for 5 minutes.
5. Now add the garlic and sauté 2 minutes.
6. Add the potatoes, salt, pepper, chili, and curry and cook for 5 minutes.
7. Add the vegetable broth, put the lid on and cook for 25 minutes, stirring occasionally.
8. When the potatoes are cooked, remove the saucepan from the grill and let it rest for 5 minutes.
9. Now put the curry potatoes on the serving plates and serve.

15 MINUTES

35 MINUTES

4

Griddle pumpkin

10 MINUTES

6 MINUTES

4

INGREDIENTS

- » 21 oz of pumpkin pulp
- » 1 tbsp of chopped rosemary
- » 1 tbsp of chopped thyme
- » Balsamic vinegar to taste
- » Olive oil to taste
- » Salt and pepper to taste

DIRECTIONS

1. Preheat the grill to 374 ° F for 10 minutes.
2. Wash and dry the pumpkin pulp and then cut it into slices.
3. Brush the pumpkin with olive oil and sprinkle the surface with salt, pepper, rosemary and thyme.
4. When the grill is ready, place the pumpkin and grill 3 minutes per side.
5. After cooking, put the pumpkin on serving plates.
6. Season with oil and balsamic vinegar and serve.

Griddle tomatoes with feta and honey

15 MINUTES

16 MINUTES

4

INGREDIENTS

- » 4 ripe tomatoes
- » 2 tbsp of honey
- » 3.5 oz of diced feta cheese
- » Salt and pepper to taste
- » Olive oil to taste

DIRECTIONS

1. First preheat the grill for 10 minutes at 356 ° F.
2. Wash, rinse and let the tomatoes dry, cutting them in half
3. Brush the olive oil over the entire surface of the tomatoes and season with salt and pepper.
4. Place the tomatoes to grill on the direct side of the grill.
5. Close the lid and cook for 8 minutes per side.
6. As soon as the tomatoes are cooked, remove them from the gas grill and let them rest for a few minutes.
7. Serve your tomatoes on a serving dish sprinkled with honey and surrounded by feta cubes.

Griddle vegetables with curry

25 MINUTES

40 MINUTES

4

INGREDIENTS

- » 1 eggplant
- » 3 zucchinis
- » 1 yellow pepper
- » 1 potato
- » 10 cherry tomatoes
- » 1 red onion
- » 1 tbsp of curry powder
- » Salt and pepper to taste
- » Olive oil to taste

DIRECTIONS

1. Preheat the grill to 374 ° F for 10 minutes.
2. Peel the onion, cut it into wedges and put it in a bowl.
3. Wash the zucchinis, dry them, and cut them into cubes. Put them in the bowl with the onion.
4. Wash the eggplant, wash it, cut it into cubes and put it in the bowl with the other vegetables.
5. Remove the cap, seeds, and white pepper strands, wash it, and then cut it into cubes.
6. Peel, wash and dice the potato.
7. Also put the potato and pepper in the bowl with the other vegetables.
8. Finally, wash the tomatoes, remove the stalk, and cut them into quarters. Mix with the other vegetables.
9. Season all the vegetables with three tablespoons of olive oil. Salt them well and flavor them with the curry.
10. When the grill is hot enough, put in a cast iron saucepan and heat it for 5 minutes.
11. Then pour the vegetables inside, add the vegetable broth and put the lid on.
12. Cook for 40 minutes, stirring occasionally.
13. After cooking, remove the saucepan from the grill and let it rest for 5 minutes.
14. Put the curried vegetables on the serving plates and serve.

Griddle soy noodles with vegetables

20 MINUTES

20 MINUTES

4

INGREDIENTS

- » 7 oz of glass noodles
- » 6 button mushrooms
- » 1 shallot
- » 1 clove of garlic
- » 1 carrot
- » 3.5 oz of spinach
- » 1 tbsp of toasted sesame seeds
- » 1 tbsp of seed oil
- » 1 tsp of sesame oil
- » Salt and pepper to taste
- » Olive oil to taste

For the dressing
- » 3 tbsp of clear soy sauce
- » 1 tbsp of dark soy sauce
- » 2 tbsp of brown sugar
- » 1 tbsp of sesame oil

DIRECTIONS

1. Soak the noodles in a bowl with hot water for an hour.
2. Start by preparing the dressing: in a bowl put the sugar, the light soy sauce, the dark one and the sesame oil. Stir until the sugar has completely dissolved and set aside.
3. Peel and wash the garlic, carrot and scallion and then cut them into thin slices.
4. Remove the earthy part of the mushrooms, wash them, dry them, and cut them into slices.
5. Wash and dry the spinach and then cut them into strips.
6. Prepare the grill for indirect heat cooking at 392 ° F.
7. Place a wok on the grill, add oil and heat for 4-5 minutes.
8. Add the seed oil and sesame oil and heat them.
9. Now add the garlic, mushrooms and shallots and sauté for 2 minutes.
10. Add the spinach and carrots and cook for 5 minutes.
11. Season with salt and pepper and now add the drained noodles.
12. Cook for 2 minutes and finally pour the sauce.
13. Stir well, sauté for 5 minutes and then remove the wok from the grill.
14. Divide the noodles into serving plates, sprinkle with the cooking juices and serve.

Griddle zucchini cheeseburger

INGREDIENTS

25 MINUTES

15 MINUTES

6

- » 3 zucchinis
- » 2 eggs, beaten
- » 3.5 oz of grated cheddar
- » 3.5 oz of breadcrumbs
- » 7 oz of flour
- » 1 tbsp of parsley
- » Salt and pepper to taste
- » 2 tbsp of olive oil

DIRECTIONS

1. Preheat the 374 ° F gas grill.
2. Peel and wash the zucchinis, then cut them into cubes.
3. Also wash the parsley, then chop finely.
4. When the grill is ready, heat a cast iron pan with olive oil and brown the zucchini cubes with a little water for about 15 minutes.
5. When they are ready, drain and mash them finely in a large bowl using a vegetable press.
6. Then transfer the zucchini puree to another bowl and add the finely grated cheddar and half the flour.
7. Incorporate the two beaten eggs and the parsley.
8. Season with salt and pepper.
9. Start forming small burgers with the zucchini filling.
10. Meanwhile mix the oil and breadcrumbs until the mixture becomes melted and crumbly.
11. Put each zucchini burger in the flour, then pass it in the eggs and then in the breadcrumbs.
12. Press the breadcrumbs onto the burgers to make sure it sticks.
13. Now put the burgers directly on the grill.
14. Cook for 15 minutes, turning them often.
15. When cooked, remove the burgers from the grill and let them rest for a couple of minutes.
16. Serve still hot with your favorite sauce.

Sauteed griddle peppers with soy sauce

INGREDIENTS

- » 1 red pepper
- » 1 yellow pepper
- » 1 green pepper
- » 2 cloves of garlic
- » 4 tbsp of olive oil
- » 1 tbsp of soy sauce
- » 1 tsp of sugar
- » ½ glass of brandy
- » Salt and pepper to taste

DIRECTIONS

1. Preheat the grill to 356 ° F.
2. Remove the cap, the seeds, and the white filaments from the peppers, then wash them repeatedly under running water, drain and cut them into strips.
3. Peel the garlic cloves and then cut them into slices.
4. Put the wok on the grill, add the oil and heat for 5 minutes.
5. Now add the garlic and sauté for 2 minutes.
6. Now add the peppers, season with salt and pepper and cook for 1 minute.
7. Now put the lid on the wok and cook for 20 minutes, stirring occasionally.
8. Then add the soy sauce, sugar, and deglaze with the brandy.
9. Cover the wok again and cook for another 15 minutes.
10. After cooking, remove the wok from the grill and let it rest for a couple of minutes.
11. Now put the peppers and the cooking juices in the serving plates and serve.

15 MINUTES

40 MINUTES

4

Soft griddle potato pie

15 MINUTES

24 MINUTES

4

INGREDIENTS

- » 21 oz of boiled potatoes
- » 10.5 oz of cream cheese
- » 1.4 oz of grated parmesan cheese
- » 2 eggs
- » 2 spring onions
- » 1 tbsp of dried marjoram
- » Butter to taste
- » Salt and pepper to taste

DIRECTIONS

1. Preheat the grill to 356 ° F for 10 minutes.
2. Meanwhile, peel the potatoes and cut them into thin slices.
3. Remove the rootlets and 2/3 of the green part of the spring onions. Cut them into thin slices.
4. Take a cast iron saucepan and brush the bottom with butter.
5. Put the spring onions, cream cheese, parmesan, salt, pepper, eggs, and marjoram in a bowl and mix everything well.
6. Put the mixture on the bottom of the saucepan and then lay the potatoes on top.
7. Cover the saucepan, close the grill lid, and cook, indirectly, for 20 minutes.
8. After cooking, remove the saucepan from the grill and let it rest for 10 minutes.
9. Now divide the pie into 4 parts, put it on serving plates and serve.

Vegetarian griddle Kebab Skewers

20 MINUTES
+ 2 H REST

15 MINUTES

4

INGREDIENTS

» 12.3 oz of Tofu cheese
» 7 oz of Greek yogurt
» 1 green pepper
» 1 red pepper
» 1 tbsp of grated fresh ginger
» A pinch of curry powder
» A pinch of turmeric powder
» ½ glass of olive oil
» ½ tablespoon of spicy paprika
» 2 tablespoons of lemon juice
» Salt and pepper to taste

DIRECTIONS

1. First, take the tofu and cut it into cubes.
2. Now wash the vegetables, removing the stalk of the peppers and the peel of the onions.
3. Cut the vegetables into pieces.
4. Put the yogurt and spices (turmeric, curry, paprika and ginger) in a bowl.
5. Add the cheese and vegetables to the yogurt and leave to marinate for 2 hours in the fridge.
6. After the two hours, preheat your grill for 10 minutes at 356 ° F.
7. Prepare the skewers by alternating the various marinated ingredients.
8. Place the skewers on the grill, close the lid and cook for 15 minutes.
9. Meanwhile, pour the marinade into a bowl and season with salt and pepper.
10. Mix well with a fork.
11. While the skewers are cooking, brush them generously with the sauce.
12. Turn the skewers a couple of times to get even cooking.
13. Remove the skewers from the barbecue and serve with the spiced yogurt marinade sauce.

Aromatic tuna steak and grilled pepper sauce

20 MINUTES

35 MINUTES

4

INGREDIENTS

- » 1 21.1 oz tuna fillet
- » 3 tbsp of breadcrumbs
- » 1 tbsp of grated Parmesan cheese
- » 1 red pepper
- » 1 yellow pepper
- » 1 bunch of chopped basil
- » 1 bunch of chopped parsley
- » The grated zest of 1 lemon
- » Olive oil to taste
- » Salt and pepper to taste
- » 1 lemon zest

DIRECTIONS

1. Preheat the grill to 356 ° F for 10 minutes.
2. Wash and dry the peppers.
3. When the grill is ready, place the peppers and grill them for 20 minutes, turning them often.
4. As soon as the peppers are cooked, remove them from the grill and place them in a bowl.
5. Wash and dry the tuna fillet.
6. Put the breadcrumbs, Parmesan, lemon zest, salt, pepper, basil, parsley in a bowl and mix everything well.
7. Brush the tuna with olive oil and then roll it into the mix of herbs and breadcrumbs.
8. Place the tuna on the grill and cook for 2 minutes on each side.
9. Once cooked, put the tuna on a cutting board and let it rest for a few minutes.
10. Meanwhile, peel the peppers, cut them into cubes and put them in a bowl.
11. Season them with oil, salt and pepper and then put them on serving plates.
12. Cut the tuna into slices, put them on plates with the peppers and serve.

Griddle cod fillets with mint sauce

INGREDIENTS

» 4 cod fillets of 7 oz each
» ½ glass of milk
» 12 mint leaves
» 1 cup of cooking cream
» 2 limes
» 1 tsp of paprika
» Salt and pepper to taste
» Olive oil to taste

DIRECTIONS

1. Preheat the grill to 410 ° F for 10 minutes.
2. In the meantime, remove the bones and skin from the cod fillets, wash them and then dry them.
3. Wash and dry the mint leaves and put them in the mixer.
4. Add the milk and cooking cream and blend until you get a smooth sauce.
5. Take 4 sheets of aluminum foil and brush them with olive oil.
6. Put the cod fillets inside and season with oil, salt, pepper, and the filtered lime juice.
7. Sprinkle with the mint sauce and close the foil.
8. Place the parcels on the grill and close the lid.
9. Cook for 20 minutes.
10. After cooking, remove the fish from the grill and let it rest for a few minutes.
11. Carefully open the packets so as not to burn yourself with the steam, put the contents on the serving plates and serve.

TIPS: I recommend that you combine this recipe with Griddle soy noodles with vegetables

20 MINUTES

20 MINUTES

4

Griddle noodles with shrimp

25 MINUTES

15 MINUTES

4

INGREDIENTS

- » 8.8 oz of noodles
- » 20 shrimp
- » 1 medium-sized zucchini
- » 10 mint leaves
- » 2 chopped red chilies
- » 2 limes
- » 4 tbsp of soy sauce
- » 2 tbsp of sesame seed oil
- » Salt taste
- » 2 tbsp of tamarind paste
- » Salt and pepper to taste
- » Olive oil to taste

DIRECTIONS

1. Put the noodles in a bowl with boiling water and let them soak for 30 minutes.
2. Preheat the grill to 356 ° F.
3. Wash the zucchini and then cut it into thin slices.
4. Put the chilies in a bowl with the sesame oil, lime juice, soy sauce and tamarind paste. Mix well until you get a smooth sauce.
5. Shell the prawns, remove the black filament, then wash them and let them drain.
6. Put the wok with a little olive oil on the grill and let it heat for 5 minutes.
7. When the wok is hot, add the prawns and zucchini, season with salt and pepper and sauté for 5 minutes.
8. Add the drained noodles and the sauce and cook for 5 minutes.
9. Once cooked, remove the wok from the grill and place the noodles on serving plates.
10. Sprinkle with the cooking juices and serve.

Griddle salmon with ginger

20 MINUTES + 30' REST

10 MINUTES

4

INGREDIENTS

» 4 salmon steaks
» 1 lemon
» ½ glass of dry Sherry
» 3 tbsp of soy sauce
» 1 tbsp of seed oil
» 2 tsp of fresh ginger
» Salt and pepper to taste

DIRECTIONS

1. Put the Sherry, the filtered lemon juice, the soy sauce, the seed oil, the ginger, salt, and pepper in a bowl.
2. Mix until you get a homogeneous emulsion.
3. Wash the salmon steaks, remove the bones, and place them in the bowl with the marinade.
4. Refrigerate and marinate for 30 minutes.
5. After 30 minutes, preheat the grill to 356 ° F for 10 minutes.
6. When the grill is ready, place the salmon skin side up.
7. Cook for 5 minutes on each side, often brushing the fish with the marinade.
8. When the salmon is cooked, remove it from the grill, place it on serving plates and serve.

TIPS: I recommend that you combine this recipe with Griddle vegetables with curry

Griddle salmon with herb crust

15 MINUTES

20 MINUTES

4

INGREDIENTS

- » 4 salmon steaks
- » 2 tbsp of chopped parsley
- » 1 tbsp of chopped fennel
- » The grated zest of 1 lemon
- » 2 minced garlic cloves
- » Breadcrumbs to taste
- » Salt and pepper to taste
- » Olive oil to taste

DIRECTIONS

1. Place the griddle on the grill and preheat to 392 ° F.
2. Wash and dry the salmon steaks and remove all the bones present.
3. Pour the chopped herbs into a bowl and add the breadcrumbs, grated lemon zest, salt, pepper and 4 tablespoons of olive oil. Mix everything well.
4. Season the salmon fillets with salt and pepper and place on the hot plate on the skin side.
5. Put the breading on the salmon, close the grill lid and cook for 20 minutes.
6. Once cooked, remove the salmon from the grill, place it on serving plates and serve.

TIPS: you can combine with Vegetarian griddle Kebab Skewers

Griddle sea bass with potatoes

20 MINUTES

20 MINUTES

4

INGREDIENTS

» 4 sea bass fillets of 7 oz each
» 1 clove garlic
» 2 bay leaves
» 2 sage leaves
» ½ glass of white wine
» 1 tbsp of mixed spices
» 28.2 oz of boiled potatoes
» 1 sprig of rosemary
» Salt and pepper to taste
» Olive oil to taste

DIRECTIONS

1. Preheat the grill to 392 ° F for 10 minutes.
2. Meanwhile, wash the sea bass fillets and remove all the bones.
3. Peel the potatoes and then cut them into thin slices.
4. Wash sage, bay leaf and rosemary and then chop them.
5. Peel and wash the garlic and then chop it.
6. Brush a griddle with olive oil and place it on the grill.
7. Put the potatoes on top of the griddle, the sea bass and season with oil, salt and pepper.
8. Sprinkle with the garlic and chopped herbs, deglaze with the wine and close the grill lid.
9. Cook for 20 minutes.
10. After cooking, remove the fish from the grill and let it rest for a few minutes.
11. Now put the sea bass fillets and potatoes on the serving plates and serve.

Griddle sea bream with lime and coriander

15 MINUTES

25 MINUTES

4

INGREDIENTS

- » 4 sea bream fillets of 10.5 oz each
- » 2 tbsp of soy sauce
- » 1 tsp of brown sugar
- » 1 tsp of grated fresh ginger
- » 3 minced garlic cloves
- » 2 tsp of coriander seeds
- » 5 limes
- » Salt and pepper to taste
- » Olive oil to taste

DIRECTIONS

1. lace the griddle on the grill and preheat to 356° F for 10 minutes.
2. Wash and dry the sea bream fillets and remove all the bones present.
3. Wash and dry the limes, grate the zest, and squeeze the juice into a bowl.
4. Add salt, pepper, sugar, soy sauce, garlic, and coriander seeds to the bowl with the lime juice. Mix until a homogeneous emulsion is obtained.
5. When the griddle is hot enough, put the sea bream fillets on the skin side and sprinkle them with the emulsion.
6. Close the lid, and cook for 25 minutes, turning the fish halfway through cooking.
7. After cooking, remove the fish from the grill, put it on serving plates and serve.

TIPS: you can combine with Griddle pineapple upside down pie

Griddle sea bream with oranges and fennel

INGREDIENTS

- » 4 sea bream fillets of 8.8 oz each
- » 2 oranges
- » 1 fennel
- » 1 tbsp of saffron
- » 1 tbsp of fennel seeds
- » 1 tsp of green peppercorns
- » Salt and pepper to taste
- » Olive oil to taste

DIRECTIONS

1. Preheat the grill to 392 ° F for 10 minutes
2. Wash and dry the sea bream fillets and remove all the bones present.
3. Wash and dry the oranges, squeeze half an orange into a bowl and cut the others into thin slices.
4. Emulsify 2 tablespoons of extra virgin olive oil with saffron, fennel seeds, green pepper and orange juice.
5. Remove the beard and the outer leaves of the fennel, then wash it and cut it into thin slices.
6. Brush a baking pan with olive oil and put the orange slices and fennel slices inside.
7. Season with oil, salt and pepper and then put the sea bream fillets on top.
8. Season the sea bream with salt and pepper and then sprinkle with the emulsion.
9. Put the pan on the grill, switch to indirect cooking, close the lid and cook for 20 minutes.
10. After cooking, remove the pan from the grill and let it rest for 5 minutes.
11. Now put the sea bream, orange slices and fennel on the serving plates and serve.

25 MINUTES

20 MINUTES

4

Griddle tuna in aromatic sauce

PREPARATION: 15 MINUTES
COOKING: 10 MINUTES
PORTIONS: 4

INGREDIENTS

» 4 tuna steaks of 7 oz each
» 2 tbsp of chopped parsley
» 4 spring onions
» 2 cloves of garlic
» 2 lemons
» 1 sprig of tarragon
» Olive oil to taste
» Salt and pepper to taste
» Pink pepper powder to taste

DIRECTIONS

1. Preheat the grill to 356 ° F for 10 minutes.
2. Squeeze and strain the lemon juice into a bowl.
3. Peel and chop the garlic cloves.
4. Put the garlic, 5 tablespoons of olive oil, salt, pepper, 1 glass of water and parsley in the bowl with the lemon juice.
5. Stir until you get a homogeneous emulsion and then set aside.
6. Wash the tarragon and then chop it.
7. Brush the tuna steaks with olive oil, season with salt, pink pepper, and the tarragon.
8. When the grill is ready, put the tuna in and grill 3 minutes per side.
9. After cooking, remove the tuna, pour the emulsion into a saucepan, and place it on the grill.
10. Bring the emulsion to a boil and then remove it from the grill.
11. Put the tuna fillets on serving plates.
12. Sprinkle them with the emulsion and serve.

TIPS: For a fish-based lunch or dinner, I recommend combining this recipe with Salmon griddle shish kebab

Salmon griddle shish kebab

PREPARATION: 25 MINUTES
COOKING: 15 MINUTES
PORTIONS: 4

INGREDIENTS

» 28.2 oz of salmon fillet
» 7 oz of eggplant
» 7 oz of yellow peppers
» 7 oz of zucchinis
» 6 cherry tomatoes
» 1 lemon
» 1 tbsp of dried oregano
» 1 tbsp of chopped marjoram
» 7 oz of Greek yogurt
» 1 sprig of thyme
» Salt and pepper to taste
» Olive oil to taste

DIRECTIONS

1. Wash and dry the salmon fillet, remove skin and bones and then cut it into cubes.
2. Wash and dry the peppers, zucchinis and eggplant and cut them into cubes.
3. Wash and dry the cherry tomatoes and then cut them in half.
4. Take the skewers and put the zucchini first, then the salmon, then the pepper, salmon, eggplant, salmon and tomato.
5. Proceed in the same way for the other 11 skewers.
6. Preheat the grill to 392 ° F for 10 minutes.
7. Meanwhile, put 4 tablespoons of olive oil, the filtered lemon juice, oregano, salt, pepper and marjoram in a bowl and mix well.
8. Brush the skewers with the marinade.
9. Oil the grill and place the skewers on top.
10. Close the lid and cook for 15 minutes, turning the skewers from time to time and brushing with the marinade.
11. Meanwhile, add the yogurt, salt, pepper, and thyme and mix until you get a homogeneous mixture.
12. Once cooked, place the salmon shish kebabs on the plates.
13. Sprinkle with the yogurt sauce and serve.

TIPS: If you want to combine something sweet with this recipe you can do it with Griddle chocolate muffins

Griddle apple muffins

20 MINUTES

20 MINUTES

4

INGREDIENTS

- » 1 tbsp of baking powder
- » 3 eggs
- » 9 tbsp of flour
- » 9 tbsp of plain yogurt
- » 9 tbsp of granulated sugar
- » 3 apples
- » 9 tbsp of olive oil
- » Powdered sugar to taste

DIRECTIONS

1. Preheat the grill to 356 ° F for 10 minutes.
2. Shell the eggs in a bowl and add the sugar.
3. Whip the eggs and sugar with an electric mixer until you get a light and fluffy mixture.
4. Now add the yogurt and oil and continue whipping.
5. Finally, add the baking powder and flour and continue mixing until you get a smooth and lump-free mixture.
6. Peel the apples, remove the seeds, cut them into cubes and put them in the dough.
7. Stir until the apples are completely incorporated.
8. Place the cups inside the baking pan for muffins.
9. Pour the mixture into the cups and place the pan on the grill.
10. Close the lid and cook for 20 minutes.
11. Check the cooking with a toothpick and, if they are cooked, remove them from the grill, otherwise continue cooking for another 5 minutes.
12. Once cooked, remove the baking pan from the grill and let the muffins cool.
13. Once cooled, remove the muffins from the baking pan, sprinkle with powdered sugar and serve.

Griddle Banana Bread

INGREDIENTS

- » 3.17 oz of butter
- » 4 oz of granulated sugar
- » 2 eggs
- » 1 tsp of vanilla extract
- » 8.8 oz of flour
- » 1 tbsp of baking powder
- » 2 large, ripe bananas
- » 1 orange
- » 1 tsp of cinnamon powder
- » A pinch of salt

DIRECTIONS

1. Put the butter and sugar in a bowl and mix, with an electric mixer, until you get a soft and homogeneous cream.
2. Add the eggs and continue mixing.
3. Now add the vanilla, grated orange zest, salt, cinnamon, and baking powder.
4. Stir and when you have obtained a homogeneous mixture, add the flour.
5. Chop the bananas, put them in a deep plate and mash them with a fork, reducing them to puree.
6. Finally, add the bananas and mix until you get a compact and lump-free mixture.
7. Brush a plumcake mold with olive oil and put the mixture inside.
8. Preheat the grill to 356 ° F and, when it reaches temperature, put the mold inside.
9. Close the lid and cook for 40 minutes.
10. After 40 minutes, check the cooking by inserting a toothpick in the center of the cake: it must come out perfectly dry.
11. If the banana bread is cooked, remove it from the grill and let it cool.
12. Once cold, cut it into slices and serve.

25 MINUTES

40 MINUTES

4

Griddle blueberry muffins

20 MINUTES

25 MINUTES

6

INGREDIENTS

- » 8.8 oz of flour
- » 3.5 oz of granulated sugar
- » 1 sachet of baking powder
- » ½ teaspoon of baking soda
- » 1 pinch of salt
- » 8.8 oz of plain yogurt
- » 3 tbsp of whole milk
- » 1 egg
- » 4 tbsp of seed oil
- » 5.2 oz of blueberries

DIRECTIONS

1. Preheat the grill to 356 ° F.
2. Put the flour, baking powder, baking soda, sugar and salt in a bowl and mix.
3. In another bowl, mix all the milk, yogurt, lightly beaten egg and seed oil.
4. Wash and dry the blueberries.
5. Now add the liquid ingredients to the solid ones.
6. Stir until you get a smooth, lump-free mixture.
7. Finally add the blueberries and mix everything well.
8. Place the cups inside the muffin mold.
9. Pour the mixture into the cups and place the mold on the grill.
10. Close the lid and cook for 25 minutes.
11. After 25 minutes, check the cooking with a toothpick and, if the muffins are not yet cooked, continue cooking for another 5 minutes.
12. Once cooked, remove the mold from the grill and let the muffins cool completely.
13. When they are cold, remove the muffins from the mold and serve.

Griddle chocolate muffins

20 MINUTES

30 MINUTES

6

INGREDIENTS

» 2.8 oz of flour
» 1 oz of unsweetened cocoa
» 3.1 oz of brown sugar
» 1 egg
» ½ glass of milk
» 0.52 oz of melted butter
» 1 teaspoon of baking powder
» 1 pinch of salt
» 3.5 oz of dark chocolate

DIRECTIONS

1. Preheat the grill to 356 ° F.
2. Put the flour, baking powder, cocoa, sugar, and salt in a bowl and mix well.
3. In another bowl, mix all the milk, lightly beaten egg and melted butter.
4. Combine the liquid ingredients with the solid ones and mix quickly until you get a homogeneous and lump-free dough.
5. Chop the dark chocolate, set aside a small part, and add the rest to the mixture, stirring for a minute.
6. Place the cups inside the muffin mold and sprinkle with the remaining chocolate.
7. Put the muffin tin on the grill, close with the lid and cook for 20 minutes.
8. Once cooked, remove the mold from the grill and let the muffins cool.
9. As soon as the muffins are cold enough, remove the muffins from the mold and serve.

Griddle pineapple upside down pie

PREPARATION: 20 MINUTES
COOKING: 50 MINUTES
PORTIONS: 8

INGREDIENTS

» 8.8 oz of flour
» 5.2 oz of soft butter
» 3.5 oz of granulated sugar
» ½ glass of whole milk
» 3 eggs
» ½ vanilla bean
» The zest of half a lemon
» 1 tsp of baking powder
» 7 slices of pineapple in syrup

for the caramel:
» 5.2 oz of granulated sugar
» ½ glass of water
» 1 tbsp of butter

DIRECTIONS

1. Preheat the grill to 356 ° F.
2. Put the sugar, water, and butter in a round baking pan.
3. When the grill is hot, put the baking pan and melt the butter and sugar.
4. Remove the baking pan from the grill and set aside.
5. In a bowl, whip the soft butter together with the sugar, lemon zest and vanilla seeds with an electric mixer. Whip until you get a light and fluffy mixture.
6. Add an egg and mix until completely incorporated.
7. Do the same with the other egg.
8. Incorporate the sifted flour together with the baking powder and mix with a spatula from bottom to top so as not to dismantle the dough.
9. Finally add the milk and finish mixing.
10. Now drain the pineapple slices and place them on top of the caramel.
11. Pour the dough into the baking pan and place it on the grid.
12. Close the lid and cook for 40 minutes.
13. When the cake is cooked, take it out of the oven and let it rest for 1 minute and then turn it upside down on a serving plate.
14. Let the cake cool, cut it into slices and serve.

Gluten free griddle carrot cake

15 MINUTES

30 MINUTES

6

INGREDIENTS

- » 1 glass of carrot juice
- » 3.5 oz of sugar
- » ½ glass of seed oil
- » 7 oz of rice flour
- » 1.7 oz of potato starch
- » 1.7 oz of almond flour
- » 1 tbsp of baking powder
- » 1 tbsp of sliced almonds

DIRECTIONS

1. Preheat the grill to 356 ° F.
2. Put the carrot juice, oil, and sugar in a bowl.
3. Beat with an electric mixer for 5 minutes.
4. Incorporate the flours, baking powder and sliced almonds and mix until you get a homogeneous and lump-free mixture.
5. Brush a round baking pan with olive oil and pour the dough inside.
6. Put the baking pan on the grill, close the lid and cook for 30 minutes.
7. Check the cooking with a toothpick and, if the cake is not cooked yet, continue cooking for another 5 minutes.
8. After cooking, remove the baking pan from the grill and let the cake cool.
9. When the cake is cold, you can cut it into slices and serve it.

Griddle gluten-free bread with pumpkin

**20 MINUTES
+ 2 H REST**

45 MINUTES

1 LOAF

INGREDIENTS

- » 17.6 oz g of gluten-free flour mix
- » 10.5 oz of steamed pumpkin
- » 1 glass of water
- » ½ tsp of dry yeast
- » 1 tbsp of olive oil

DIRECTIONS

1. Put the flour mix, baking powder and pumpkin in a bowl. Mix everything with an electric mixer for 5 minutes.
2. Now add the oil and continue to knead until you get a smooth and homogeneous mixture.
3. Form the dough into a ball, cover the bowl with a kitchen towel and let it rise for 2 hours.
4. After two hours, put a little gluten-free flour on a work surface and put the dough on top.
5. Work it for 10 minutes and then make cuts on the surface.
6. Preheat the grill to 482 ° F.
7. Brush a cast iron saucepan with olive oil and heat it on the grill.
8. When the saucepan is hot, put the dough inside, close the saucepan with the lid and cook for 45 minutes.
9. After 20 minutes, lower the grill temperature to 446 ° F.
10. After cooking, remove the saucepan from the grill and let it rest for 15 minutes.
11. Remove the bread from the pan and, when it has cooled, cut it into slices and serve.

Griddle gluten-free muffin with apples and coconut

INGREDIENTS

- » 5.2 oz of rice flour
- » 1.7 oz of cornstarch
- » 1.7 oz of coconut flour
- » 3.5 oz of sugar
- » 1 glass of water
- » The grated rind of an orange
- » ½ glass of seed oil
- » 1 apple
- » 1 tbsp of baking powder
- »

DIRECTIONS

1. Preheat the grill to 356 ° F.
2. Put the oil, water, and sugar in a bowl. With an electric mixer, whisk until the sugar has completely dissolved.
3. Add the flour, cornstarch, coconut flour and baking powder and mix until smooth.
4. Take the muffin mold and put the cups inside and then fill them with the dough.
5. Peel the apple, remove the seeds, cut it into cubes and place them on top of the dough.
6. Put the mold on the grill, close the lid and cook for 25 minutes.
7. Once cooked, remove the mold from the grill and let the muffins cool.
8. When the muffins have cooled, remove them from the mold, sprinkle the surface with a little coconut flour and serve.

20 MINUTES

25 MINUTES

4

Griddle gluten-free pancakes with Greek yogurt and fresh fruit

PREPARATION: 20 MINUTES
COOKING: 15 MINUTES
PORTIONS: 10 PANCAKES

INGREDIENTS

- » 5.2 oz of gluten-free flour
- » 2 eggs
- » 1 glass of milk
- » 1 oz of melted butter
- » 1 tbsp of sugar
- » 1 pinch of salt
- » 1 tsp of baking powder
- » 3.5 oz of Greek yogurt
- » 3.5 oz of fresh fruit
- » 4 tbsp of honey

DIRECTIONS

1. Place the griddle on the grill and preheat to 392 ° F for 10 minutes.
2. Meanwhile, sift the flour, sugar, salt and yeast into a bowl.
3. In another bowl, break the eggs, add the milk and melted butter and beat with a fork.
4. Now combine the two compounds and mix well with an electric mixer, to form a smooth and lump-free batter.
5. Now grease the griddle and then pour over a ladle of mixture.
6. Cook for 2 minutes on each side and then add another ladle of batter.
7. Proceed in the same way up to the end of the ingredients.
8. Once cooked, divide the pancakes into serving plates.
9. Put the Greek yogurt in a bowl and add the honey.
10. Mix well for a few minutes and then pour the mixture over the pancakes.
11. Add your favorite fruit and serve.

Griddle gluten-free pizza with potatoes and speck

PREPARATION: 20 MINUTES
REST TIME: 1 HOUR 30 MIN
COOKING: 25 MINUTES
PORTIONS: 2 PIZZAS

INGREDIENTS

» 8.8 oz of gluten-free flour mix
» 1 tbsp of olive oil
» 1 pinch of salt
» 2 tbsp of dry yeast
» 1 glass of warm water
» 3.5 oz of mozzarella
» 2 potatoes
» 15 slices of speck
» 1 tbsp of chopped rosemary

DIRECTIONS

1. Mix the flour mix together with the dry yeast and oil in a bowl.
2. Gradually add the lukewarm water and knead until a homogeneous and lump-free mixture is obtained.
3. Shape the dough into two balls, cover the bowl with a kitchen towel and let it rise in the heat for at least 1 hour and 30 minutes.
4. Meanwhile, peel and wash the potatoes then cut them into thin slices.
5. After the rising time, take the dough and roll it out until it forms two discs.
6. Brush the surface of the dough with olive oil.
7. Then arrange the finely sliced potatoes and the mozzarella cut into slices, add salt and pepper, brush them with oil and spread over the chopped rosemary.
8. Preheat the grill to 392 ° F.
9. When the grill has reached temperature, put on the pizza plate and heat for 10 minutes.
10. After 10 minutes, place the pizza and close the lid.
11. Cook for 25 minutes.
12. After cooking, remove the pizza from the grill and place the slices of speck on top.
13. Cut the pizza into 4 parts and serve.

Griddle meatballs with sauce

20 MINUTES

35 MINUTES

4

INGREDIENTS

- » 14 oz of ground minced meat
- » 2 tbsp of breadcrumbs
- » 1 tbsp of grated Parmesan cheese
- » 1 egg
- » 1 tbsp of chopped parsley
- » 1 pinch of grated nutmeg
- » 10.5 oz of tomato puree
- » ½ glass of water
- » Dried oregano to taste
- » Salt and pepper to taste
- » Olive oil to taste

DIRECTIONS

1. Preheat the grill to 392 ° F.
2. Meanwhile, put the meat in a bowl.
3. Add the egg, salt, pepper, breadcrumbs, parmesan, and parsley and knead until you get a homogeneous mixture.
4. With the mixture obtained, go to form a total of 24 spheres.
5. Put the cast iron pan on the grill and heat 2 tablespoons of olive oil.
6. Place the meatballs and sauté for 5 minutes.
7. Add the tomato puree, add the water, oregano, salt, and pepper and close with the lid.
8. Cook for 20 minutes, stirring occasionally.
9. Once cooked, remove the meatballs from the grill and let them rest for 5 minutes.
10. Put the meatballs and the sauce on the serving plates and serve.

Griddle Rainbow pancakes

INGREDIENTS

- » 10.5 oz of flour
- » 1 glass of milk
- » 1 egg
- » 4 tbsp of honey
- » Mixed food colors

DIRECTIONS

1. Place the griddle on the grill and preheat it to 392 ° F.
2. Meanwhile, pour the flour into a bowl and add the egg, and with the help of an electric mixer, mix everything well.
3. Add the milk slowly, until it is completely incorporated.
4. Now divide the mixture into many small bowls, first add a pin of color, stir with a spoon, and add more color, until you have the consistency you want.
5. When the griddle is hot enough, oil it and then start cooking the pancakes.
6. Cook for two minutes on each side, then remove them from the grill and put them on plates.
7. Sprinkle with honey and serve.

15 MINUTES

10 MINUTES

4

Griddle fruit skewers covered with chocolate

15 MINUTES

12 MINUTES

4

INGREDIENTS

- » 2 bananas
- » 12 strawberries
- » 1 kiwi
- » 2 tbsp of sugar
- » 3.5 oz of dark chocolate

DIRECTIONS

1. Preheat the grill to 356 ° F for 10 minutes.
2. Peel the bananas and cut them into slices that are not too thin.
3. Wash and dry the strawberries.
4. Peel the kiwis and then cut them into cubes.
5. Put the skewers together. First put a strawberry, then the kiwi and finally the banana.
6. Proceed in the same way until the end of the fruit.
7. Sprinkle with sugar and place the skewers on the grill.
8. Cook for 12 minutes, turning the fruit often.
9. Put the dark chocolate in a saucepan and let it melt, stirring constantly to prevent it from burning.
10. When the skewers are cooked, remove them from the grill and place them on serving plates.
11. Sprinkle with dark chocolate and serve.

Griddle fruit skewers with colorful sprinkles

20 MINUTES

30 MINUTES

4

INGREDIENTS

» 35 oz of mixed fruit: strawberries, pineapple, kiwi, bananas, melon, watermelon, apples, pears
» 10 tbsp of sugar
» 8 mint leaves
» 4 raspberries
» Colored sugars to taste

DIRECTIONS

1. Preheat the grill to 392 ° F for 10 minutes.
2. Wash and dry the strawberries and then cut them in half.
3. Wash and dry the pineapple pulp and then cut it into cubes.
4. Peel the bananas, peaches, apples, pears and then cut them into cubes.
5. Wash and dry the melon and watermelon pulp, remove all the seeds, and then cut them into cubes.
6. Take 8 steel skewers and place the fruit cubes alternately.
7. Sprinkle the fruit with sugar.
8. When the grill is hot enough, place the skewers and cook for 12 minutes.
9. Turn the skewers often and, when ready, remove them from the grill and place them on plates.
10. Sprinkle with colored sprinkles and serve.

Griddle waffle with egg and spinach

10 MINUTES

20 MINUTES

4

INGREDIENTS

- » 4 salty waffles
- » 4 eggs
- » 14 oz of spinach leaves
- » 5.2 oz of fresh spreadable cheese
- » Salt to taste
- » Olive oil to taste

DIRECTIONS

1. Preheat the grill to 356 ° F.
2. Wash and dry the spinach.
3. When the grill has reached temperature, place a cast iron pan on top and heat 1 tablespoon of olive oil.
4. When the oil has heated up, add the spinach and sauté for 5 minutes.
5. Season with salt and then remove the spinach.
6. Now add the eggs, season with a little salt and cook for 6 minutes.
7. Remove the pan from the grill and put the waffles on.
8. Heat them for 2 minutes on each side and then remove them from the grill and put them on the plates.
9. Spread the cheese on the waffles, add the spinach and finally the eggs and serve.

Alternative ingredients

After showing you the recipes, I want to give you some alternative ingredients that you can use to create many other recipes starting from the ones I have included.

Let's start with the alternatives to flour. Below I will give you a list of flours that you can use instead of 00 flour:

- Rye flour, spelled, millet and other whole grains.
- Rice flour.
- Legume flours.
- Quinoa flour.

- Oat flour.
- Millet flour.
- Corn flour.
- Barley flour.
- Kamut flour.

As for the bacon, you can replace it with:

- Raw ham.
- Speck.

- Baked ham.
- Prague cooked ham.

As for Cheddar, I recommend replacing it with:

- Swiss.
- Edamer.

- Emmenthal.
- Mozzarella cheese.

As for the meat recipes that I have described to you, in all the recipes you can use the alternatives you prefer, the important thing is that you adjust the times and temperatures as I have included in the tables.

Plus, if you prefer a vegan alternative, I recommend replacing meat and fish with tofu, tempeh or seitan.

As for sauces, the choice is endless: you can use mayonnaise, cocktail sauce, tartar sauce, Hollandaise sauce, Pico de Gallo sauce, ketchup, bbq sauce, guacamole or Aioli sauce.

CONVERSION TABLE

In this section of the book, I have included some conversion tables, which I hope will be useful for you to understand how to adjust the various measures of the ingredients you are going to use.

16 TABLESPOONS = 1 CUP

12 TABLESPOONS = 3/4 CUP
10 TABLESPOONS + 2 TEASPOONS = 2/3 CUP
8 TABLESPOONS = 1/2 CUP

6 TABLESPOONS = 3/8 CUP
5 TABLESPOONS + 1 TEASPOON = 1/3 CUP
4 TABLESPOONS = 1/4 CUP

2 TABLESPOONS = 1/8 CUP   1 TABLESPOON = 1/16 CUP
2 TABLESPOONS + 2 TEASPOONS = 1/6 CUP   3 TEASPOONS = 1 TABLESPOON

ALL-PURPOSE FLOUR AND CONFECTIONERS' SUGAR (ICING OR POWDERED SUGAR)

CUPS TO GRAMS

1/8 CUP=15 GRAMS   5/8 CUP=70 GRAMS
1/4 CUP=30 GRAMS   2/3 CUP=75 GRAMS
1/3 CUP=40 GRAMS   3/4 CUP=85 GRAMS
3/8 CUP=45 GRAMS   7/8 CUP=100 GRAMS
1/2 CUP=60 GRAMS   1 CUP=110 GRAMS

GRANULATED, SUPERFINE OR CASTER SUGAR

CUPS TO GRAMS

1/8 CUP=30 GRAMS   5/8 CUP=140 GRAMS
1/4 CUP=55 GRAMS   2/3 CUP=150 GRAMS
1/3 CUP=75 GRAMS   3/4 CUP=170 GRAMS
3/8 CUP=85 GRAMS   7/8 CUP=200 GRAMS
1/2 CUP=115 GRAMS   1 CUP= 225 GRAMS

LIGHT, GOLDEN OR DARK BROWN SUGAR

CUPS TO GRAMS

1/8 CUP=25 GRAMS   5/8 CUP=125 GRAMS
1/4 CUP=50 GRAMS   2/3 CUP=135 GRAMS
1/3 CUP=65 GRAMS   3/4 CUP=150 GRAMS
3/8 CUP=75 GRAMS   7/8 CUP =175 GRAMS
1/2 CUP=100 GRAMS   1 CUP= 200 GRAMS

CAKE FLOUR

CUPS TO GRAMS

1/8 CUP= 10 GRAMS   2/3 CUP= 65 GRAMS
1/4 CUP= 20 GRAMS   3/4 CUP= 70 GRAMS
1/3 CUP= 25 GRAMS   7/8 CUP= 85 GRAMS
3/8 CUP= 30 GRAMS   1 CUP= 95 GRAMS
1/2 CUP= 50 GRAMS
5/8 CUP= 60 GRAMS